Ilia Celiento

essays by

Laura Andreini
zio Carpenzano
Luca Galofaro
Franco Purini

ON THE ROAD city
Rome

ON THE ROAD
Editor of collection
Laura Andreini

editorial project
Forma Edizioni srl, Florence, Italy
redazione@formaedizioni.it
www.formaedizioni.it

editorial direction
Laura Andreini

author
Ilia Celiento

editorial staff
Maria Giulia Caliri
Livia D'Aliasi
Andrea Benelli
Beatrice Papucci

graphic design
Isabella Peruzzi

translations
Katy Hannan

photolithography
LAB di Gallotti Giuseppe Fulvio,
Florence

texts by
Laura Andreini
Orazio Carpenzano
Luca Galofaro
Franco Purini

Ilia Celiento: pp. 28-37, 48-85, 88-117,
124-129, 134-137, 140-151, 162-163,
168-169, 174-177, 180-185, 192-209
Concetta Tavoletta: pp. 38-47, 118-123,
130-133, 152-161, 170-173, 186-191

Ilia Celiento is an architect, and PhD candidate in Project Design and Theory at the Architectural Faculty of the Sapienza University in Rome. She is also Teaching assistant at the Faculty of Architecture and Industrial Design at the University of Campania.

First Edition: November 2019

ISBN 978-88-55210-15-7

Table of contents

Guidebook as tool

On the Road is a collection of contemporary architecture guidebooks whose purpose is to tell about a place, whether a city or larger area, through its architectural works chosen to be visited and experienced directly.

The guidebook has a convenient special jacket that opens into a map marking the location of the architectural works and interesting sites to visit. On the back are miniature images and addresses of the architectural works described in detail within.

The book starts with short essays explaining the city or area's present day and history and outlining possible future scenarios with planned or imminent projects. Each work features a photograph of the whole, an architectural drawing (plan or section), a short description, and facts including architect, type, year of construction, address, website, and how to visit it.

The finest architecture of each city and suggested routes are represented by this collection of not-to-be-missed, "timeless" buildings that uniquely define their settings. General information and useful tips for travelers help them optimize their visits and quickly understand the essence of the place described.

Museums, theatres, restaurants, hotels and a list of top architectural firms working in the city let visitors turn a regular trip into an opportunity for study or work.

Note: The pinpoints outside the maps at the beginning of the itineraries are viewable on the rear of the book jacket.

Rome

Laura Andreini*

During the planning of this book, part of the On the Road series, dedicated to Rome, we realised that we were describing a city, or rather, a metropolis, that has a surreal quality of timelessness. In order to 'read' Rome, visitors have to dig through its many layers and anachronisms before they can understand and reconsider a concept of contemporaneity which, in this city more than any other, is completely relative. Everything coexists as if it has endured with similar traits for time immemorial.

If, on one hand, there are certain positive aspects, where contemporary architecture seems to be incorporated easily within the previous urban fabric, on the other, all transformations and new structures seem to have appeared almost unnoticeably, and the quality of these interventions has not often received due recognition. For this reason, a guide to contemporary architecture in Rome seemed particularly crucial.

The Italian capital is extremely complex. It contains many unresolved problems and multiple identities: the museum stature of Rome is interwoven with its political status, the religious context extends irregularly, while the city of parks and green spaces coexists with, but without infiltrating the suburbs, the result of widespread building speculation. Each 'city' has its own identity and history, which often seem to exist on parallel lines but without ever crossing one another. Contemporary architects find themselves having to work in extremely difficult situations, but which are also stimulating and like no other context. The examples in this book demonstrate the challenges and success of many projects and their designers.

This guide to Rome is divided into 4 stimulating itineraries leading from the historic city centre, continuing north, then moving to the eastern suburbs, to finish in the southern area in the EUR district, an essential stop for a global vision of Roman architecture. The proposed routes do not only travel through physical space, but also through time, and this is one of the most obvious characteristics of the eternal city. Everything exists in an urban overlaying, providing visitors with a rich and unique panorama. For example, on leaving the centre, moving northwards, visitors leave the Roman Forum to stroll through a quarter from the early 20th century, il Flaminio, to be then confronted by Zaha Hadid's MAXXI museum, in a dialogue with the famous sports arena by Pierluigi Nervi, not far from the Auditorium del Parco della Musica by Renzo Piano. Even in its contemporary aspects, Rome asserts its identity as a city that is entirely unique.

* Laura Andreini, Architect and Associate Professor at DIDA, University of Florence. Co-founder of Studio Archea where she still works, she is also writer and Deputy Editor for *area* magazine.

Political / geographical facts

country
Italy

language
Italian

area code
+39 06

coordinates
41°53' 35" N
12°28' 58" E

area
496.3 sq mi

population
2,873.494

density
5,790 sq mi

time zone
UTC+1

city website
www.comune.roma.it

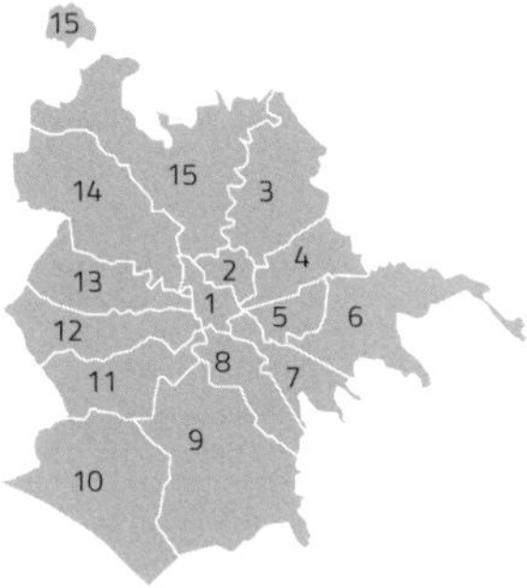

Administrative districts

1. Municipality Rome I
2. Municipality Rome II
3. Municipality Rome III
4. Municipality Rome IV
5. Municipality Rome V
6. Municipality Rome VI
7. Municipality Rome VII
8. Municipality Rome VIII
9. Municipality Rome IX
10. Municipality Rome X
11. Municipality Rome XI
12. Municipality Rome XII
13. Municipality Rome XIII
14. Municipality Rome XIV
15. Municipality Rome XV

General information
useful addresses and numbers

INFORMATION OFFICES*

www.turismoroma.it
tel +39 06 0608

Tourist Infopoint Termini
Stazione Termini, via Giovanni Giolitti 34
daily / 8 am - 6.45 pm

Tourist Infopoint Castel Sant'Angelo
Piazza Pia
daily / 9.30 am - 7 pm

Tourist Infopoint Fori Imperiali
Via dei Fori Imperiali
daily / 9.30 am - 7 pm

Tourist Infopoint Fiumicino
Aeroporto Leonardo Da Vinci –
Arrivi Internazionali Terminal T3
daily / 8.00 am - 8.45 pm

EMERGENCY SERVICES

Carabinieri 112
Police 113
Fire Department 115
Emergenza Sanitaria 118

URBAN TRANSPORT*

Bus and Tram
tickets can be bought from automatic vending machines in metro stations, on surface means of transport, or from sales points at tobacconists, news stands, and authorised bar-cafés.
muoversiaroma.it
www.atac.roma.it

Metro (3 lines)
tickets can be bought from automatic vending machines in metro stations, on surface means of transport, or from sales points at tobacconists, news stands, and authorised bar-cafés.
muoversiaroma.it
www.atac.roma.it

Taxi
Cooperativa Radiotaxi 3570: +39 06 3570
Servizio CHIAMATAXI: +39 06 06 09
Taxi Roma Samarcanda: +39 06 55 51
Pronto Taxi: +39 06 66 45
www.apptaxi.it/roma

Car sharing
Car Sharing Roma, Car2go, Enjoy, Share'ngo

Bike sharing
Bici&Baci, BikeByBus, Sharewood, BikeAway

GENERAL CONSULATE OF UNITED STATES OF AMERICA
Via Vittorio Veneto, 121 – 00187 Rome (RM)
Contact centre +39 06 46741

GENERAL CONSULATE OF CHINA
Via Bruxelles, 56 – 00198 Rome (RM)
Contact centre +39 06 84413458

BRITISH CONSULATE
Via Conte Rosso, 25 – 00185 Rome (RM)
Contact centre +39 06 77255775

GENERAL CONSULATE OF FRANCE
Via Giulia, 251 – 00186 Rome (RM)
Contact centre +39 06 68601500

RUSSIAN EMBASSY IN ITALY
Via Nomentana, 116 – 00161 Rome (RM)
Contact centre +39 06 44235625

HOW TO PHONE

from a local landline: dial local code number followed by phone number (06)

from a foreign landline: dial international code (+39) city code (06) and phone number

* Ticket categories:
BIT ticket (standard), 10-BIT ticket, 24Hr ticket, 48Hr ticket, 72Hr ticket, CIS ticket (7 days), public transport passes

Useful tips

1. Rome offers a wide range of **accommodation** from luxury hotels frequented by the international and Roman jet set, like the **Grand Hotel de la Minerve**, a 17th century palace renovated by the architect, Portoghesi, a short stroll from the **Pantheon/10**, **Piazza Navona**, **Trevi Fountain/11** and the **Piazza di Spagna/04**, that offers magnificent views from its Minerva Roof Garden. Hidden away in the smaller streets, there are elegantly renovated B&B apartments for every budget. **YellowSquare** is an innovative hostel option: it offers bunk beds, guided tours of the city, communal spaces for small events, yoga sessions, cooking lessons, a hair styling experience, and fashion contests.

2. The Roman **transport** system covers a wide area and the **subway** is the quickest way to travel. It has only two lines (A) red line and the (B) blue, which branches to a second B1 line. The subway trains run every day from 5.30 am to 11.30 pm, and until 1.30 am on Saturdays. During daytime hours, visitors can admire the city using one of the numerous **bus** lines that also leave from Termini Station. We advise getting there early for bus travel. Alternatively, the no. 8 and no. 2 tram lines are efficient and well connected between the city centre and city limits. **Car-sharing** and **bike-sharing** services are also available. For the ecologically-minded, there are 78 **e-hubs** for renting electric bikes to visit surrounding areas. E-hubs are generally at the major transport interchange points.

3. Rome is a city of **art**, **culture**, **films**, and **music**. From September, **museums** and **theatres** open the new exhibition and events season. Most sites attract a vast number of visitors on the first of May, the Notte dei Musei (19-20 May) when museums are open at night, and on European heritage Days (29-30 September). The **MAXXI/39** by Zaha Hadid and the **MACRO/48** by Odile Decq are contemporary museums that have been exhibiting new forms of culture for 15 years, like the latest reconversion masterpiece by Jean Nouvel, **Palazzo Rhinoceros/21**, that houses wonderful art pieces. Ancient sites like the **Castel Sant'Angelo/26**, **Imperial Forum**, and the **Baths of Caracalla**, regularly host artistic and cultural events. Rome holds wonderful **events** and **festivities** all year long directed by renowned professionals. For movie lovers, the season starts in March with **Cinemente** at the **Palazzo delle Esposizioni/13**. At the same time, the **Casa del Cinema** shows previews of short films during the **Irish Film Festival Film**, followed by the **Festival of New French Cinema**, and **New European Cinema**. The cycle continues with **Spanish Cinema** in May, and travels all over Italy; this is followed by the magnificent **David di Donatello** awards night. The season concludes in autumn with the great **Festa del Cinema di Roma**, with international stars on the red carpet. A blend of every type of music can be heard at the **Festa della Musica** on June 21st, every year. A few days later, the Fondazione Musica per Roma holds the opening night of the **Roma Summer Fest**, at the **Auditorium Parco della Musica/37**: 2 months of concerts with the world's top rock and pop stars, great jazz musicians and singer-songwriter stars. Concerts by international and Italian musicians, are hosted at other sites like the **Circus Maximus** which has launched a cutting edge project to promote the site with augmented and virtual reality technology.

4. Water remains the natural element that has always been a major feature in Rome. Cast iron drinking fountains called **"nasoni"**, can be found at every street corner and piazza for fresh water, especially during the summer. Water nourishes and enriches the green spaces, **parks** and **gardens** of Rome. To visit some of the famous **villas**, underground parking is available at **Villa Borghese/46**, where the exit leads visitors through a park of different tree species, before reaching the **Borghese Gallery**. To return to the centre, there is a wonderful walk down the hill from the Pincio terrace. Nearby, in the Nomentano area, there is a traditional **Italian Liberty style garden** at **Villa Torlonia**, while **Villa Ada** has lush green English gardens. A short distance from the **Colosseum/19** and **Palatino**, the wonderful **Villa Celimontana** park is a glorious place to stop and rest. Some amazing Roman aqueduct architecture can be seen in the **Parco degli Acquedotti** and the **Parco della Caffarella**, both part of the **Parco Regionale dell' Appia Antica**. On the other side of the Tiber, magnificent fountains decorate the gardens of **Villa Dora Pamphili**, one of the largest villas in Rome. From the **Giardino degli Aranci**, an enchanting green space in the Aventino hills, there are breathtaking views of the dome of St. Peter's.

5. To visit Rome, you need at least a week, not because of its size, but because Rome is best discovered strolling along its winding narrow streets. Rome is passionate, nostalgic, and romantic: a city where you do not need to look for tourist attractions, but because it is enough to just sit on the steps of some church or historic palace to soak up the history. Rome is a city where you will often meet unexpected people. Strolling along **Trastevere** you will see a Swedish woman shopping at her favourite green grocers, an American student on a bicycle, young lovers sharing a meal in the ghetto, an elderly lady buying little objects at the **market in Porta Portese**, before you get lost among the market stalls in **Campo de' Fiori**. Late in the afternoon, you might come across government ministers and lawyers chatting in the **Goccetto** wine bar in via Giulia, or maybe simply stop and enjoy the sunset from the **Caffarelle terrace** in the Capitoline Museums. Follow the home cooking aromas, and stop at one of the small shops in **via Cola di Rienzo** and **via del Corso**, then visit the new **Rinascente** department store in via del Tritone and admire the interior decor by young designers, before deciding to splurge on one of the famous designer brands in **via Condotti**.

Rome. Echoes, illusions, aspirations

Orazio Carpenzano*

Rome is a *book* that tells of foundations events, a mosaic of different realities. An endless variety of identities and an extraordinary mass of cells that have generated architectural and urban fabrics.

This is how the city is perceived by scholars, and instinctively, by inhabitants. This is how it has been represented throughout history in the endless descriptions and views of those who have admired it.

This is how the city is perceived by scholars of its modern and contemporary history, from the transformations since 1870, when it became the capital of the new State of Italy, during its rapid growth following World War Two, up to the present day.

Rome begins its third millennium still maintaining the incredible continuity that has endured throughout its long history.

It did not yet appear like this in Giambattista Nolli's magnificent map, which represented his fourteen *rioni* with such accuracy and impeccable expression that the city was recognisable at first glance thanks to his wonderful topographic and geo-spatial structure.

However, it did exist in the famous engraving by Giovan Battista Piranesi, based on the Severan Marble Plan: a huge archipelago, its morphological evidence arranged in juxtaposition, but all converging towards an image that was defined, but split, broken into discordant pieces, all trying to anchor themselves in the overall picture, despite the unstable and uncertain spatial coordinates.

A figural complexity that, like a prophecy, announced the destiny of Rome, that even today, still flees from the idea of formal reconstruction.

Therefore, it is appropriate to face the difficult task of creating a city guide using a kind of paratactic device, incomplete, free from the temptation of an improbable narrative of its origins, in an attempt to create an ideal web of different routes, explorations, each one independent and rich in its own personal interpretation, and to reveal the necessary choices (even for publishing purposes) and consequential observations for some form of collation, an exchange, a comparison among spatial concepts, objects and wonderful itineraries, all co-existent, all contemporary, yet all different in space and time.

Rome presents itself with countless possible identities and documentary evidence, beginning with the unsolved complications of its status as a museum, political, and religious city, and a city in a powerful environmental situation.

In short, it reflects the daily exchange of the city's multiple facets. To quote an expression dear to urban planners, Rome finds it very hard to hold together its ancient stones, its landscapes and its citizens (inhabitants).

Rome inspires creation, it stimulates the desire for new projects. It is a city, whose incredible palimpsests constantly evoke overwriting, geopsychic layers to be incorporated in that unusual list of artifacts, issues, and events that nestle within the city in the form of dense piles of the material and immaterial.

Rome became stratified by selecting and metabolizing types and elements from afar, in both space and time, to create a surreal heap of forms and styles that do not have the slightest influence on its illusive character. The whole world perceives Rome as the very definition of the historic city. It is a city impossible to define, and hard to describe, even for those who have studied it for many years, still posing endless questions. It is horizontal, widespread.

A gigantic outdoor space sliced up and made uneven by its wonderful, indifferent, cynical and cruel geography; in spite of its amazing architecture and the damage created by senseless speculation, in spite of the passivity and indifference of the Romans, it renews its protohistoric, primordial nature. A geography that continuously regurgitates the choices endured, the attempts to dominate it, and yet, still today, it maintains its sea, its woods, and river, ready to convert its urban future to enclose it within feasible environmental strategies.

A metropolis that awaits repairs, bridges to connect the conurban islands of endless suburbs in abandoned environments, vast plains of countryside rich in buried treasures of natural and mineral archaeology that coexist to obstruct any form of progress.

Architecture in conflict with archaeology, urban housing in a battle with farmland, culture clashing with nature, memory struggling with the future, development projects in conflict with the sense of discomfort and loss.

Rome is never enthusiastic, there is rarely a strong reaction, not even when the city is covered with insults, because to a certain extent it permits itself and others the right to incompetence.

A wonderful city that demands a truly serious reason before it will move from its passivity, its inertia, using a strict minimum of words to express anything, even to give something a name. Rome expresses "different" sense of time. Time that is suspended, repeated.

Rome is the matrix and testimony of almost every type of architecture within the city and in most parts of the world.

For this reason, it has become essential for Rome to express a renewed urban culture, completely distinct from radical comparisons or confutations, using project paradigms to re-examine its resources and reflect on the criticality of the situation without cynicism. It is also essential that the past, the present and the future coexist in the ideas and images that claim to interpret, and communicate this culture, to continue to preserve and pass it on to the world.

* Orazio Carpenzano is a full professor in Architectural and Urban Design at the Faculty of Architecture at the Sapienza University in Rome. He is Head of the Department of Architecture and Project Design, and director of the ArchiDIAP portal as well as the DIAP PRINT book series. His projects have been published internationally, and he has written articles for renowned Italian and international magazines and publications.

Rome, a city without a memory

Luca Galofaro*

> It is easier to design cities for the future than for those with a past. Rome is an interrupted city because we stopped envisaging what it could be and instead, we began to design it (badly). The main question with Rome, is time rather than space [...]. Unlike space, which is opaque, time is transparent; swimming just under the surface of the water, monuments appear like rocks, ruins like coral branches. It is the transcendent city that Bernini and Borromini had imagined [...].
>
> Giulio Carlo Argan, *Roma Interrotta*, Officina Edizioni, Rome, 1978

Rome should be considered like a city without time or memory, it should be read through its stratifications and anachronisms. The idea of 'contemporary' is a relative concept here. Walking through the streets is a unique opportunity to learn how little planning has gone into this city. Because planning in Rome is a very difficult task; this can be seen by the relatively few buildings constructed in the last ten years. But it is important to understand however, how the city has always been a model for a contemporary project.

In his book, *Towards an Architecture,* Le Corbusier entitled a chapter: *The Lesson of Rome.* The Swiss architect understood the role of Rome's ancient ruins, its buildings, its landscape, its empty spaces, and the question of time. He constructed some of his future urban visions after studying the layout of Rome. Rome teaches, but does not absorb, according to Ludovico Quaroni: "The lesson that Rome can teach is precisely this: everything disappears and everything remains, as we prefer; large things are small, and vice versa. In this context, for us, the spirit of the city has never remained unrelated to architectural or town planning projects, when these have represented the political, cultural, or artistic interpretation of a period, a situation, or of an environment, but it has been betrayed every time the intervention itself has presumed to resolve the problems of the city [...]"[1].

1 L. Quaroni, *L'immagine di Roma*, Editori Laterza, Bari, 1969

In his *L'immagine di Roma*, Quaroni narrates its architecture. It is through this narrative that he defines the nature of a city that has expanded through land, professional and political speculation. But he also speaks of a Rome whose beauty enslaves us, keeping us entrapped, even though there may be other places where it is possible to create architecture today; the reasons are many, and no doubt this is not the time and place to explain them.

In the light of these suppositions, we can confirm that when faced with the contemporary situation, Rome is a distracted city, a city incapable of considering the changes that are necessary. A city that is used to expanding by overlaying. But it refuses to consider the possibility of diffusing quality architecture (apart from the rare exceptions included in this book).

Rather than through what has been built, the force that emerges from this city comes from its *voids*, those spaces that have been partly planned, partly built, following the disasters it has suffered; with its assimilation of the abandoned, the ruins, and agricultural land as far as the heart of the city.

From the times of Nolli to Muñoz, from Poussin until the construction of the Appia Antica Regional Park, this city has always maintained the beauty and strength of its *setting* – its piazzas, its parks, its countryside – compared to the *edifice* – its buildings, its monuments, which are unequalled in any other city.

Because of its history and nature, Rome still appears today like an archipelago of islands in the midst of a sea of empty spaces. Voids of different kinds, some already developed for their potential – in other words, spaces that have been returned to the community – spaces that people can stroll through and enjoy, while others are still waiting to become part of this sea, able to connect instead of being separated.

Rome also delayed in deciding on extensive town planning projects that were widespread in other cities all over the world during the last century. This was for various concurring reasons: the power of land revenue that had an influence on regulations (such as the progressive transformation from the style of small single houses, traditional in many districts, to the much denser urban lifestyle in apartment buildings, or the increase in intensive housing destined for the middle and working classes), or the rich uneven morphology of the landscape (perhaps it is a feasible reason why the true Roman *suburbia* is composed of small, single family houses with gardens, both in the plains as well as towards the sea); or perhaps because the high cost of land and housing forced many inhabitants to look for larger models in the scattering of small towns that surround the city.

This panorama reveals the buildings described in this guide as contemporary architectural works reflected in ancient ruins. They are able to strongly confirm that another type of Rome is still possible, and that in fact, does exist.

By chance, or because of my persistent character, I have had the opportunity to construct small buildings in Rome that have won awards, some of which you will find in this book. Quality architecture, that hides a story and the long time required for their construction. Time is still a relative concept in this city.

These are the stories that have created the palimpsest of contemporary living, where architecture is always in the background compared to the city.

I have always considered Rome as a city that is incomplete, imperfect, illicit: perhaps not truly capable of being a capital city, incapable of controlling its relationship with history.

But this incomplete nature is also what makes it rich and different from other European capital cities. After reading these few lines, you can visit this city that has no memory for its future; and you will be ready to focus your gaze on a concept of extended time.

* Luca Galofaro is an Architect and Associate Professor at the University of Camerino. He was a founder member of the LGSMA and IaN+ firms, and won the Gold Medal at the Triennale di Milano for Italian Architecture (2006). He was a finalist in the Aga Khan Award (2013), and won the Iakov Chernikhov International Prize (2010). In 2017 and 2019 he curated the Orléans Architecture Biennale.

Rome, Roman Perspective

Franco Purini*

In the past sixty years, two town planning projects were proposed to determine the future of Rome: the first was proposed in 1962, and the second in 2008. Unfortunately, neither vision was accepted. The first project was aimed at moving directionality eastward along a new arterial road, "Asse Attrezzato", along which ministries, moved from the city centre, would have been incorporated among office blocks and urban facilities of various categories. This project would have included widespread green areas to reflect a modern version of the Roman countryside. The second idea consisted of providing suburban areas, which were lacking in public community spaces, with eighteen urban centralities. These should have galvanised the construction of an exclusively residential urban fabric where local services and spaces essential for social, cultural and recreational activities were practically non-existent. For reasons which are still not perfectly clear today, these two key ideas, as they were called until a few years ago, were not applied. Rome continued to grow with important interventions such as the Laurentino 38, the Corviale, and Tor Bella Monaca projects by talented architects such as Pietro Barucci, Mario Fiorentino and Lucio Passarelli, with an external belt of abusive districts inside and outside the Grande Raccordo Anulare (Ring Road), later legalised through a number of building initiatives supported by private enterprise which applied some remarkable variations to the fortunate architectural formula of the standard apartment building. The architectural quality of the interventions passed by law 167, was considerable, but there was a lack of upkeep; there was conflict between the expectations of the inhabitants, who belonged to the same social classes, but different in their approach to lifestyle. This resulted in little sense of community and no desire to maintain and upkeep their personal habitations. The isolation of these vast building complexes, far from the city centre, defined in their huge dimensions by the law that had controlled and regulated their construction, contributed largely to many of the problems that were impossible to resolve. Illegal districts also created numerous difficulties related to their shortcomings, in addition to the anarchic development, that resulted far greater than any urban prediction. The private residential fabric had not taken into consideration the rich tradition of the Roman apartment building, which apart from a few cases, was reduced to a mere distributive and volumetric layout, a deterioration, probably due to its previous success.

In spite of this rather complicated situation, many excellent architectural and constructive projects were created in recent decades, even though most Romans, including the well-educated, do not consider these buildings as having made an important contribution to the historic city centre. In fact, it is only in the last 3 or 4 decades that the EUR has been recognised as an important urban area for the quality of its 20th century architecture, not only in Rome, but all over the world. The same applies to the Sapienza University of Rome, and the E42, a project coordinated by Marcello Piacentini. Even the bad reputation linked with the INA-CASA neighbourhoods built after the war, like the Tuscolano and Tiburtino projects, the first by Mario De Renzi and Saverio Muratori, the second by Ludovico Quaroni and Mario Ridolfi, is more closely linked with social reasons than with an interpretation of urban spaces and architectural expression, very important aspects in both cases. The apartment buildings built in the fifties, early sixties and early seventies, were not considered as architecture worthy of attention until the last few decades.

The widespread lack of regard for modern architecture in the capital is partly caused by Rome's historical reputation, which, given its legendary prestige, has led towards marginalizing the present and the future with each era. This is also due to strong ideological criticism of private constructors, and to a persistent and provincial comparison between Rome and other European cities. A comparison which, especially in the historical-critical views adopted by prominent figures such as (among many others) Leonardo Benevolo, Italo Insolera, Antonio Cederna, who, in the evolution of 19-20th century architecture, identified only mistakes, flaws and speculative extremes in a series of obstinate and often unjustified preconceptions. As well as these historiographic incidents, or perhaps also with their support, for several decades the opinions concerning Rome were very negative. In 1974 Cardinal Ugo Paoletti organised a Meeting entitled On the Evils of Rome. Coincidentally, the following year, a book *Contro Roma* – was reproduced and published last year with new interventions – in which many Roman, non-Roman and foreign intellectuals painted an extremely dramatic portrait of the capital. From that time until now, with the exception of the Left-wing governments and mayors, Giulio Carlo Argan, Luigi Petroselli, Francesco Rutelli and Walter Veltroni, the notion of a disastrous collapse of Rome has become stronger and even more widespread, based on fundamental flaws on every level. The belief that this irreversible decline, and the successive decadence in the city and its various communities, is appreciated on one hand, misunderstanding the Roman novels by Pier Paolo Pasolini, as the aesthetics of decay; and on the other, it has become useful for maintaining that same decline since it permits the creation of an emergency economy expressed in different ways.

It is a well-known fact that, without an idea of how it plans to evolve, a city cannot possess the energy to participate actively in its present situation, to prepare a future that will be increasingly more open, diverse and promising. From this viewpoint, it is not difficult to understand what the sphere of a positive transformation of Rome will be. First of all, a new relationship between ancient and contemporary must be established to offer current architecture a far greater, deeper operative space. In the global era of today, it is by no means accidental that in many cities, tourists are attracted by what is new, rather than visiting historical heritage sites, as occurs in London, Paris and Shanghai. The relationship between the various and different suburbs, and between these and the historic centre, must be changed radically as soon as possible, also keeping in mind the presence of the new Roman population from all over the world, who have been introducing innovative elements into the traditions of the capital for some time. Rather than increasing culture, since it is already considerable, the presence of culture in Rome must be recognised and shared in a more enlightened, widespread and consistent way.

On this subject, we should not forget the existence of all the State and Vatican universities in Rome and from other countries, on-line universities, research institutes, extraordinary libraries, and a dozen different academies. All these, without forgetting film production, theatre, and music.

Lastly, despite the problem of scarce and infrequent financial resources, it seems that it is impossible to delay two challenges that will require several decades. An environmental revolution is needed in the region and the city, not limited simply to the consumerist market performance promoted by the smart category, nor for those who are satisfied with sustainability understood as a superficial 'mediatic' problem, resolved with vague programs, more virtual than concrete, but that are advertised as an authentic and heroic restoration of the Roman landscape in all its aspects, from safeguarding the land, to vegetation, animal life and water systems. To quote Edoardo Persico, the second aspect involves going "back to the drawing board" to study and learn how to care for our architectural heritage, from the archaeological period through to the most recent layers of modern construction. The first aspect must be rethought in an innovative way compared to the usual system, still linked with the sense of 18th century discoveries; a heritage to be extended from the historic traces of Lazio, which is not considered as a unique and valuable legacy by most people. The second is the enormous depository of architecture, from anonymous buildings to authentic masterpieces, which until today have been studied only by authorised personnel, but which should be revealed to urban communities who can find in them, in a city that is becoming increasingly more fragmented, and in many ways absent, unknown and vital elements of their common memory and identity.

* Franco Purini, Architect, is Professor Emeritus in Architectural and Urban Composition at the Sapienza University in Rome. He has been awarded numerous prizes including the Gold Medal for Art and Culture, awarded by the President of the Republic, the Milan Triennial Medal for Lifetime Achievement, as well as Gold and Silver Plaques awarded by the UID (Union of Italian Design). He is a member of the National Academy of San Luca and the Academy of Art and Design of Florence.

tà dello Sport
Colosseum
Rhinoceros Palace
Roman Forum

Vittoriano
Giardino degli Aranci
Basilica di
Sant'Andrea della Valle

Gasometer
EUR district
Church of San Rocco all'Augusteo
La Lanterna Rome

Strategies for visiting Rome

This guide will help you tour the Eternal City and visit the large range of wonderful ancient, modern and contemporary architecture the city has to offer. The guide has been divided into four itineraries, and each route takes a couple of days to visit completely. The guide begins from the city centre, then crosses the Tiber, continues northward, and visits the districts of Nomentano and Tiburtino; it continues along the via Ostiense and the EUR districts then climbs up to the Aurelio area. All itineraries can be reached by public transport, but we recommend following the routes on foot or by bike in order to enjoy every hidden corner of the city.

Itinerary A / Rome Centre

This itinerary begins symbolically with **Piazza del Popolo/01**, the entry to the city through the ancient Roman walls. You can choose whether to continue to the historic centre, or climb the Pincio stairs and start with the second itinerary. Rome Centre is the main tourist attraction area and if you stay at the Albergo degli Ambasciatori now **Grand Hotel Palace/07** you are very close to the city's most classical and iconic monuments like the **Piazza di Spagna/04**, **Fountain of the four Rivers/09**, **Pantheon/10**, **Trevi Fountain/11**. Take a stroll as far as the **Colosseum/19**, continuing on to the **Tempietto of San Pietro in Montorio /25, Castel Sant'Angelo/26** and **St. Peter's Basilica/28**. Many of these monuments are undergoing restoration and reconstruction, combining past and present and offering contrasting aspects of art and culture. Perfect examples of ancient monuments and contemporary architecture can be seen at the **Museum of the Ara Pacis/02, Exhibition Hall, Roman Garden, Capitoline Museums/17**, the **New wing of the Vatican Museums/29** and **Egyptian Academy/45**, not to mention public buildings like the **Roma Ostiense Post Office/22** and **Casa della Gioventù in Trastevere/24**.

Itinerary B / North Rome

The area north of the city centre shows a range of different periods, beginning with the 1930s, and the construction of the **Foro Italico/34** as far as the 1960s with the **Olympic Village/36.** Close by, are examples of contemporary architecture: **Auditorium Parco della Musica/37** and **MAXXI/39**. This itinerary also includes some exciting experiments in modern residential design: **San Valentino Apartment Buildings/40**, **La Nave Apartment Building/43**, **Il Girasole Apartment Building/44**, **Papanice House/52**, **Zaccardi Apartment Building/53**. Most of these buildings can be reached from the new **Annibaliano/49** and **Jonio/50** metro stations.

Itinerary C / East Rome

The route to the east of Rome is the shortest but includes a mix of different architectural styles. It is also the tour with the most contemporary buildings that have revolutionized modern work and life styles, and form the backdrop to the **Sapienza University City/57** and the **Tiburtino District/60**. This itinerary opens with the **Roma Tiburtina Station/54**, the second local transport hub. Nearby is the **Città del Sole/55** and the **National Transplant Centre/56**. The tall building of the **New BNL-BNP Paribas Headquarters/59** contrasts with certain religious buildings like the church of **Santa Maria Josefa del Cuore di Gesù/61**, **Chiesa di Dio Padre Misericordioso/62** and the **Basilica di San Giovanni Bosco/63**. The tour closes with a visit to the Mecca of the movie industry and aspiring young talent: **Cinecittà Film Studios/64.** In the same area is one of the centres of Tor Vergata university, the **Hydrobiological Laboratories/65**.

Itinerary D / South Rome

The architectural tour of Rome concludes with the most recently developed areas with a strong focus on morphological and functional research. The area was created to host the buildings for the 1942 Universal Exposition which was not held because of the Second World War. The beauty of the architecture in this area is the result of the extreme care taken by each architect in choosing materials and contemporary functional aspects without altering the pre-existent Rational style architecture. The cultural and administrative hub has been enriched with the **The Cloud Convention Centre/78**, l'**Enterprise Spa/80**, the **Groupama Assicurazione Headquarters/82** the **The Engie Building/83** and the **Eurosky Tower/84**, today, still the tallest in Italy. This area to the south of Rome is also becoming one of the most accessible zones for artistic events hosted at the **Opificio RomaEuropa/66**, and the **Staging the Museo Centrale Montemartini/67.** A large project is also underway to redevelop a new collective community around the **Corviale/72** apartment blocks. The tour concludes with the most recent building, completed in 2019, the **IBM Headquarters Rome/86**, which can be reached only by train. It marks the beginnings of a concept focused on contemporary construction in Rome.

B
C
A2
A1
D1
D2

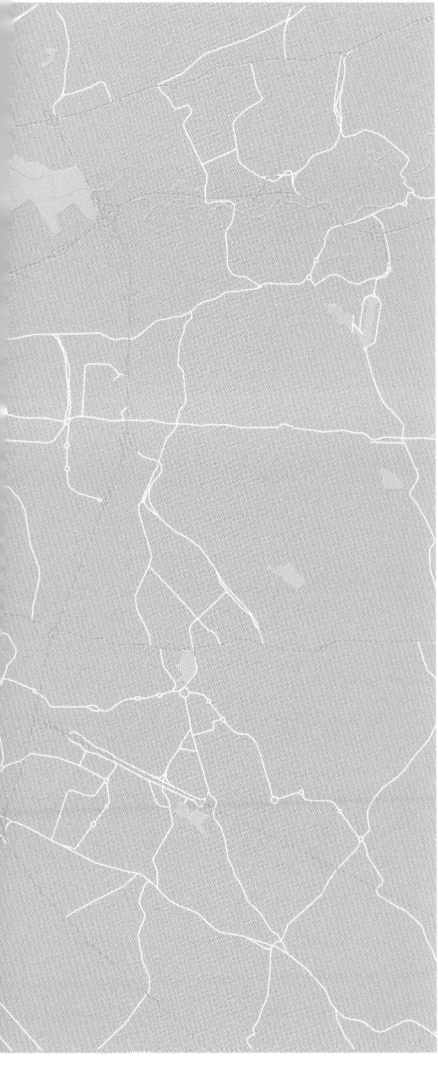

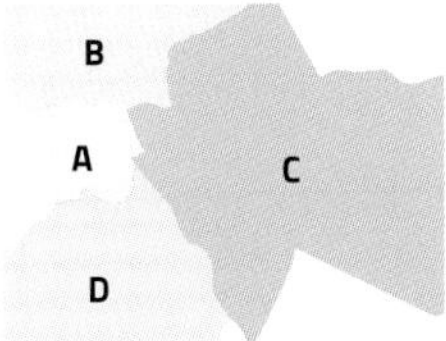

Routes

A. Rome Centre
B. North Rome
C. East Rome
D. South Rome

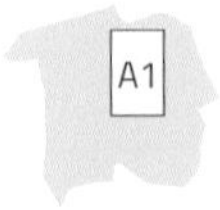

Rome Centre

01. Piazza del Popolo
02. Museum of the Ara Pacis
03. La Lanterna Rome
04. Piazza di Spagna – Fontana della Barcaccia – Spanish Steps
05. Hertziana Library – Max Planck Institute For Art History
06. Mixed Use Building
07. Albergo degli Ambasciatori and Grand Hotel Palace
08. Davide Cenci Store
09. Fountain of the Four Rivers
10. Pantheon
11. Trevi Fountain
12. Quirinale Palace and Papal Stables Renovation
13. Palazzo delle Esposizioni Restoration and Serra Piacentini Reconstruction
14. Roma Termini Railway Station
15. Restoration of the Campo Carleo "shops" and walkways at the Trajan Markets
16. Tomb of the Unknown Soldier in the Vittoriano
17. Exhibition Hall in the Roman Garden, Capitoline Museums
18. Roman Forum
19. Colosseum

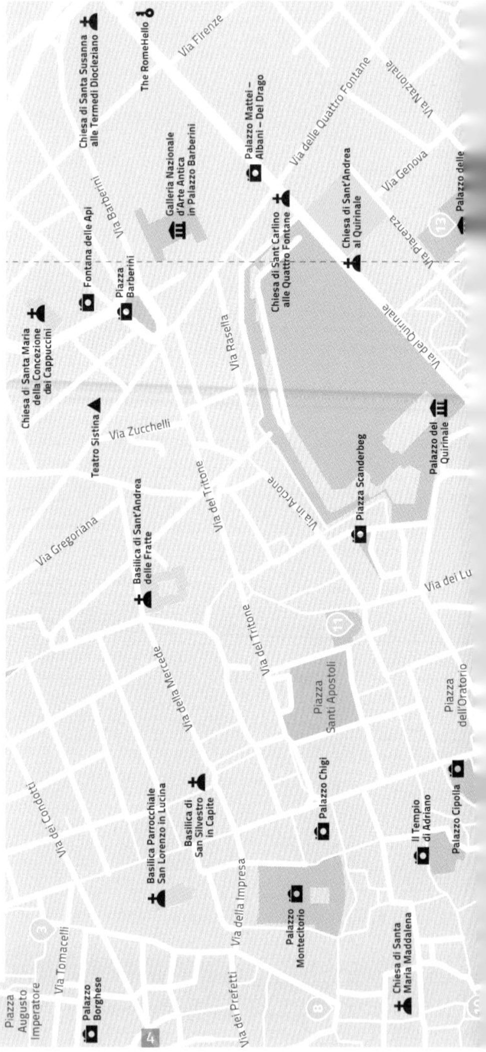

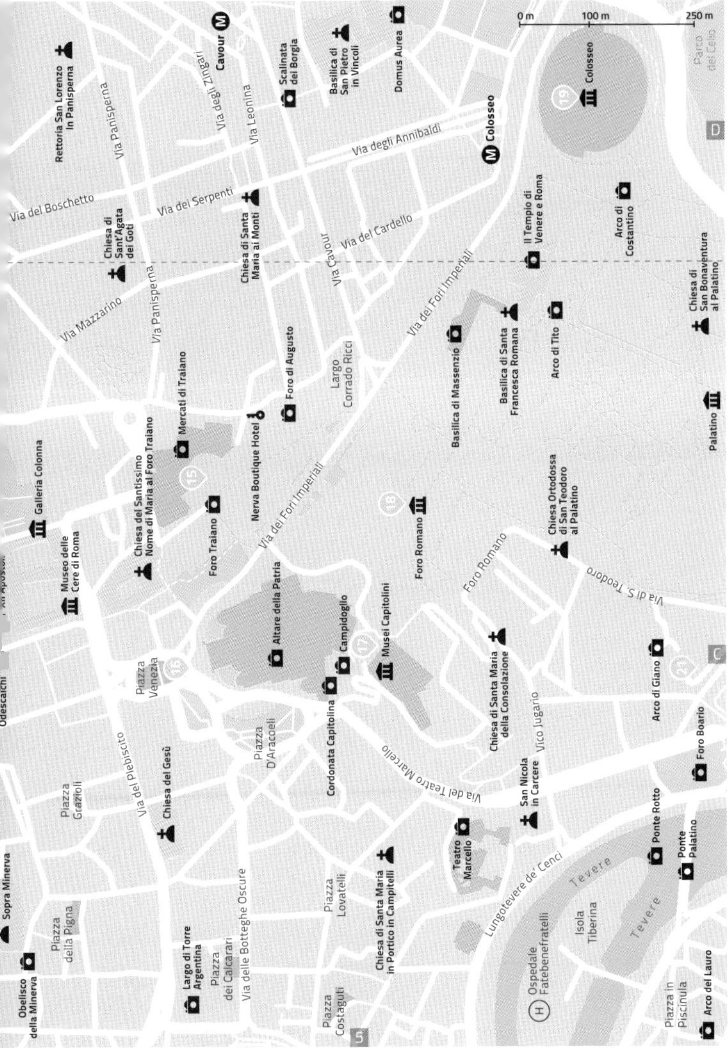

Rettoria San Lorenzo in Panisperna
Via Panisperna
Via degli Zingari
Cavour
Via Leonina
Scalinata dei Borgia
Basilica di San Pietro in Vincoli
Domus Aurea
0 m
100 m
250 m
Colosseo
Parco del Celio
Via degli Annibaldi
Colosseo
D
Via del Boschetto
Via dei Serpenti
Chiesa di Sant'Agata dei Goti
Chiesa di Santa Maria ai Monti
Via del Cardello
Via Cavour
Il Tempio di Venere e Roma
Arco di Costantino
Via Mazzarino
Via Panisperna
Via dei Fori Imperiali
Chiesa di San Bonaventura al Palatino
Basilica di Santa Francesca Romana
Arco di Tito
Foro di Augusto
Largo Corrado Ricci
Basilica di Massenzio
Mercati di Traiano
Nerva Boutique Hotel
Palatino
Galleria Colonna
Chiesa del Santissimo Nome di Maria al Foro Traiano
Via dei Fori Imperiali
Foro Romano
Chiesa Ortodossa di San Teodoro al Palatino
Museo delle Cere di Roma
Foro Traiano
Altare della Patria
Campidoglio
Musei Capitolini
Foro Romano
Via di S. Teodoro
Odescalchi
Piazza Venezia
Chiesa di Santa Maria della Consolazione
Arco di Giano
C
Via del Plebiscito
Piazza D'Aracoeli
Cordonata Capitolina
Vico Jugario
Via del Teatro Marcello
Chiesa del Gesù
Piazza Grazioli
San Nicola in Carcere
Foro Boario
Sopra Minerva
Teatro Marcello
Ponte Rotto
Ponte Palatino
Chiesa di Santa Maria in Portico in Campitelli
Piazza Lovatelli
Lungotevere de' Cenci
Tevere
Piazza della Pigna
Largo di Torre Argentina
Piazza dei Calcarari
Via delle Botteghe Oscure
Isola Tiberina
Tevere
Obelisco della Minerva
Piazza Costaguti
Ospedale Fatebenefratelli
Piazza in Piscinula
Arco del Lauro
5

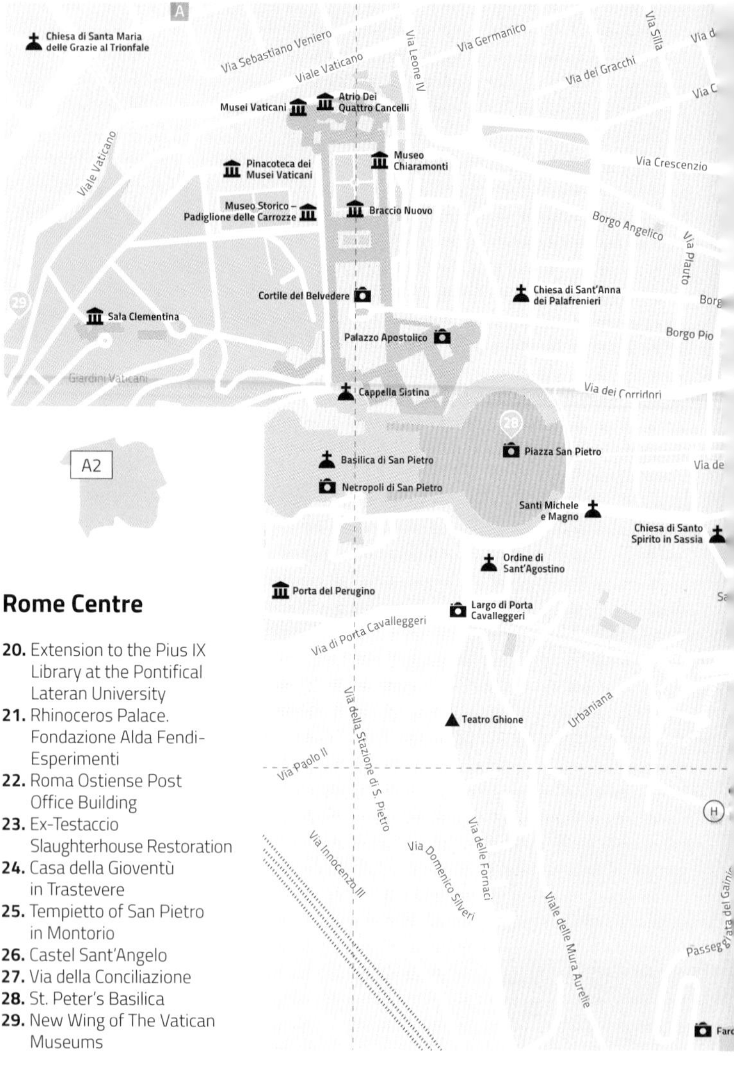

Rome Centre

20. Extension to the Pius IX Library at the Pontifical Lateran University
21. Rhinoceros Palace. Fondazione Alda Fendi-Esperimenti
22. Roma Ostiense Post Office Building
23. Ex-Testaccio Slaughterhouse Restoration
24. Casa della Gioventù in Trastevere
25. Tempietto of San Pietro in Montorio
26. Castel Sant'Angelo
27. Via della Conciliazione
28. St. Peter's Basilica
29. New Wing of The Vatican Museums

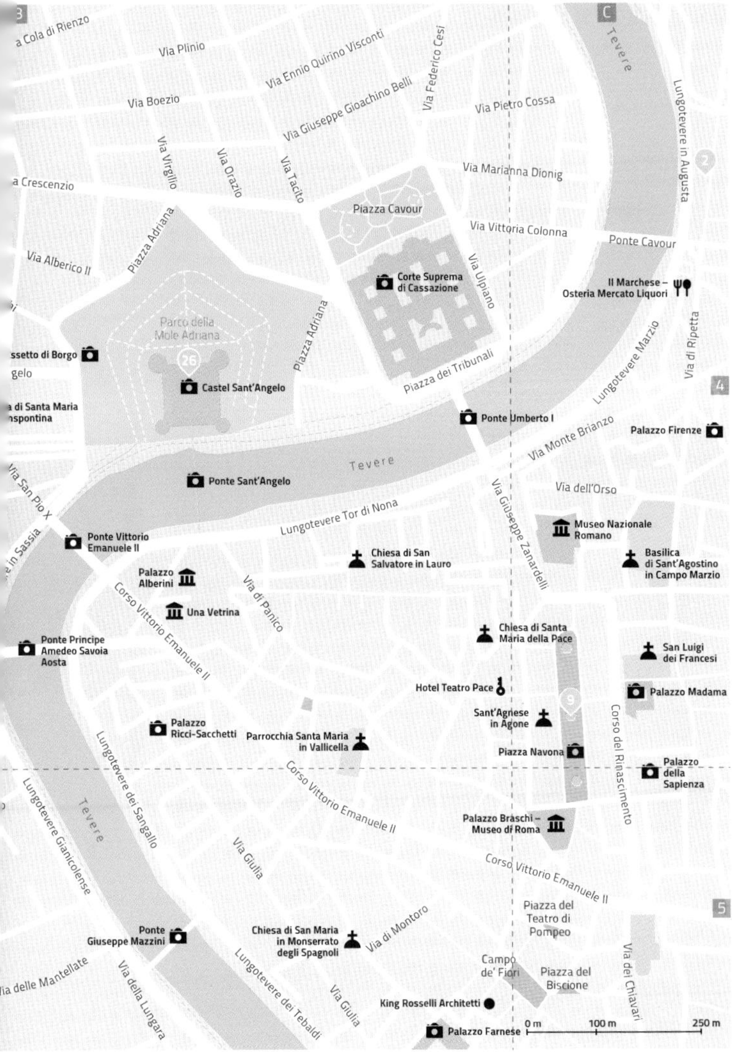
B
C
4
5
a Cola di Rienzo
Via Plinio
Via Ennio Quirino Visconti
Via Federico Cesi
Via Boezio
Via Giuseppe Gioachino Belli
Via Pietro Cossa
Tevere
Lungotevere in Augusta
Via Virgilio
Via Orazio
Via Tacito
Via Marianna Dionig
a Crescenzio
Piazza Cavour
Via Vittoria Colonna
Piazza Adriana
Ponte Cavour
Via Alberico II
Corte Suprema di Cassazione
Via Ulpiano
Il Marchese – Osteria Mercato Liquori
Parco della Mole Adriana
Piazza Adriana
Lungotevere Marzio
Via di Ripetta
ssetto di Borgo
gelo
26
Piazza dei Tribunali
Castel Sant'Angelo
a di Santa Maria
nspontina
Ponte Umberto I
Via Monte Brianzo
Palazzo Firenze
Tevere
Ponte Sant'Angelo
Via dell'Orso
Via San Pio X
Lungotevere Tor di Nona
Via Giuseppe Zanardelli
Museo Nazionale Romano
Ponte Vittorio Emanuele II
e in Sassia
Chiesa di San Salvatore in Lauro
Basilica di Sant'Agostino in Campo Marzio
Palazzo Alberini
Via di Panico
Corso Vittorio Emanuele II
Una Vetrina
Chiesa di Santa Maria della Pace
Ponte Principe Amedeo Savoia Aosta
San Luigi dei Francesi
Hotel Teatro Pace
Palazzo Madama
9
Sant'Agnese in Agone
Palazzo Ricci-Sacchetti
Parrocchia Santa Maria in Vallicella
Corso del Rinascimento
Piazza Navona
Lungotevere dei Sangallo
Palazzo della Sapienza
Lungotevere Gianicolense
Tevere
Corso Vittorio Emanuele II
Palazzo Braschi – Museo di Roma
Via Giulia
Corso Vittorio Emanuele II
Piazza del Teatro di Pompeo
Via di Montoro
Ponte Giuseppe Mazzini
Chiesa di San Maria in Monserrato degli Spagnoli
Via dei Chiavari
Via delle Mantellate
Via della Lungara
Lungotevere dei Tebaldi
Campo de' Fiori
Piazza del Biscione
Via Giulia
King Rosselli Architetti
Palazzo Farnese
0 m
100 m
250 m

01. Piazza del Popolo

piazza del Popolo
00187 Rome

external viewing only

Roma Viterbo > Flaminio

119 > Babuino / Fontanella
61 / 89 / 120F / 150F /160 / 490 / 495 / 590 / nMA > P.le Flaminio

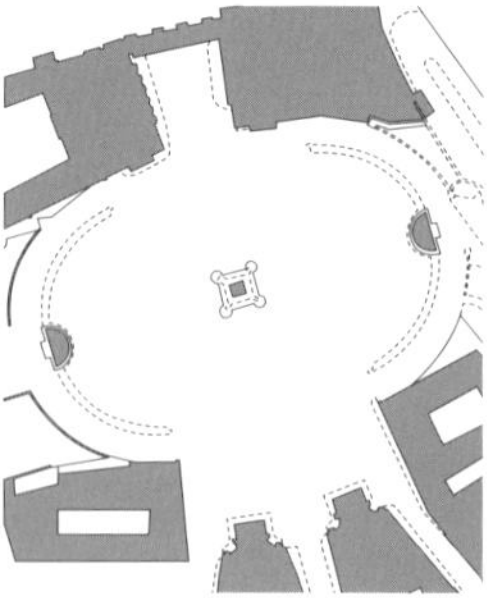

This piazza was the celebrated formal entrance to the Roman Empire and the itinerary leading to the most ancient sites of Rome. From here, the urban layout of the Trident is clearly visible, composed of via di Ripetta, via del Corso and via del Babuino. Built in 1538, the oval-shaped Piazza was designed based on two semicircular forms with a neoclassic facade designed in 1823 by Giuseppe Valadier. Over the centuries it was embellished with architectural elements, fountains and monuments. Overlooking the piazza is the Basilica of Santa Maria del Popolo restored by Gian Lorenzo Bernini, that contains some of his sculptures, works by Caravaggio, frescoes by Pinturicchio and architectural features by Raffaello. Along the southern access, in perfect symmetry, are the two 17th century churches of Santa Maria dei Miracoli and the Basilica di Santa Maria in Montesanto (the artists' church). In the centre rises the Flaminio Obelisk, symbol of Egyptian culture, 24 metres high, on a podium with four fountains featuring marble lions. Wide tree-lined ramps lead from the piazza up to the Pincio gardens, directly connecting the Pincio hill and one of the most popular terraces, a favourite place to rest during long walks.

© Luca Farinelli

architects
Giuseppe Valadier

type
public space

construction
1818

02. Museum of the Ara Pacis

lungotevere in Augusta,
via Tomacelli corner
00186 Rome

Mon - Sun /
9.30 am - 7.30 pm

+39 06 0608

info.arapacis@comune.roma.it
www.arapacis.it

A > Spagna

119 / 628 / C3 / N25 >
Augusto Imperatore
/ Ara Pacis

The Ara Pacis altar is an emblematic ancient Roman monument in white Carrara marble with carved walls depicting events from classical culture. Since 2006, the museum that houses this iconic monument, has also become home to a congress centre, a book store, a library, office and exhibition spaces. The museum is composed of three independent aligned rectangular buildings, two storeys high and 120 metres long. The travertine facades and plaster render contribute to the museum's complete integration within the urban fabric. It represents a raised loggia on a podium on the banks of the Tiber river, and sits adjacent to the Mausoleum of Augustus. A monumental stone staircase leads to the entrance in a position asymmetrical to the altar, set in the centre of a rectangular platform. Six concrete columns finished in white marble render, lead visitors into the main exhibition hall. The perfectly symmetrical glass and metal grid facades direct the light onto the altar in pure classical style in contrast with the dimmer suffused atmosphere of the entrance.

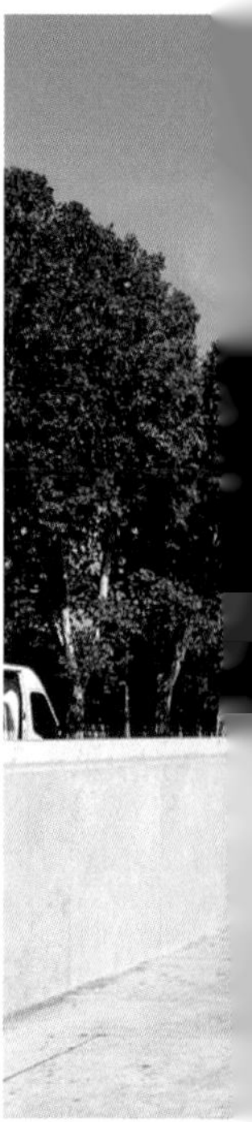

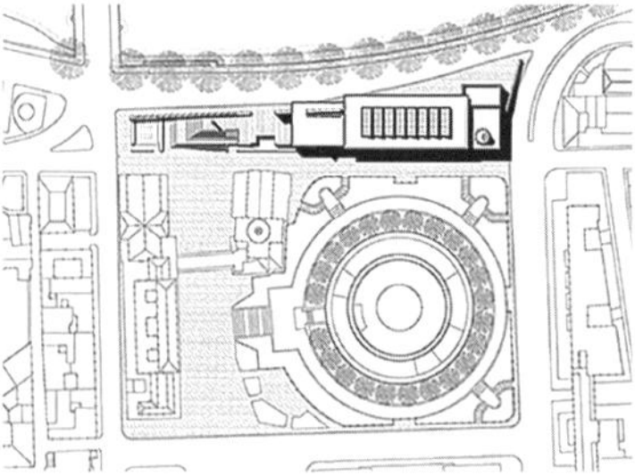

architects
Richard Meier & Partners

type
museum

construction
1995-2006

03. La Lanterna Rome

via Tomacelli 157
00186 Rome

+39 06 69377739
info@lalanternarome.it
www.lalanternarome.it

A > Spagna

85 > S. Claudio

The terrace of the ex Unione Militare building between via del Corso and via Tomacelli in Rome, houses an iconic work by Massimiliano and Doriana Fuksas. The facade of this listed building was not subject to invasive intervention; work was exclusively limited to enhancing the original lines of the building using lighting design, plus upgrades to the interior and roofing. This structure is a contemporary integration within an ancient urban context: the terrace has a panoramic view of the dome of the Basilica dei Santi Ambrogio e Carlo al Corso, while the ground floor reveals some archaeological remains of the ancient street, recently discovered and covered with glass flooring. La Lanterna is a steel and glass structure composed of triangular sections for a striking effect. Vertical connections, service spaces, accessory and technical areas intersect within the 7.5 metre height. The natural light enhances the translucent, sinuous white fibreglass interiors, while artificial led lighting illuminates the connecting spaces. The flooring on each level is a different colour: red, purple, and orange combine with the light tones casting additional colour onto the internal ceilings.

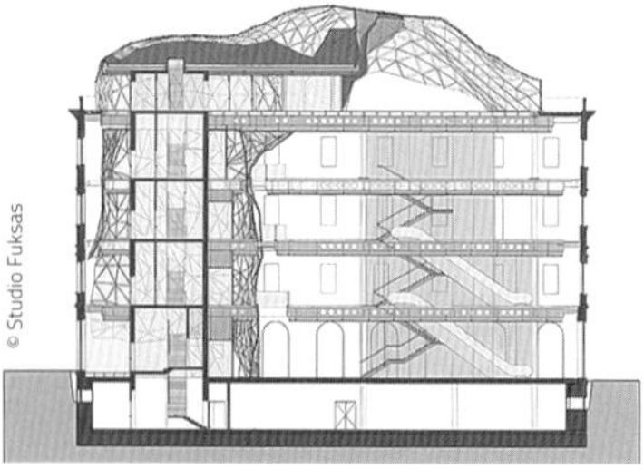

© Studio Fuksas

© Alessandra Chemollo

architects
Studio Fuksas

type
auditorium

construction
2013

04. Piazza di Spagna – Fontana della Barcaccia – Spanish Steps

piazza di Spagna
00186 Roma

external viewing only

A > Spagna

Piazza di Spagna is the embodiment of culture, history, tourism and trade. It is one of the obligatory stops during any visit to Rome. Although considered too much of a tourist site by certain purists, nonetheless, its architecture and sculpture is outstanding. Who has not stopped for a moment on the Spanish Steps below the Trinità dei Monti or posed for a photo in front of the Fontana della Barcaccia? "I will take a stroll to Piazza di Spagna", wrote Cesare Pavese: it is a sight not to be missed, the place where old friends meet up, the go-to site for models and photographers, the spot to sit for a chat and do some luxury shopping, and one of the loveliest strolls to be had in the eternal city. The Piazza is located in the so-called "English Quarter", once called Piazza di Francia, but known by its present name because it is the site of the Spanish Embassy. The famous English poet, John Keats, lived there until his death, and the area inspired some of his Romantic works. The Spanish Steps, a double ramp of 138 steps, was designed by Francesco De Sanctis, and inaugurated in 1725 thanks to a donation by a French diplomat. Hundreds of azaleas cascade down the stairs in spring, and at Christmas, garlands of lights link the piazza with the church of the Trinità dei Monti above. The Baroque architecture has undergone continuous restoration to maintain its spectacular effect. Before the stairs were built, Pietro Bernini was commissioned to create a fountain as the only monument connecting the piazza with the church. It was later completed by his son. While working on the Acqua Vergine aqueduct, the sculptor invented an excellent technical solution: he designed a boat with bow and stern, containing a small fountain in its centre, and slightly submerged in an oval pool to collect the water that overflowed from the sides of the boat and through small carved grooves. Suns and bees are the signature symbols present in all the works by the Bernini family.

architects
Fontana della Barcaccia:
Pietro and Gian Lorenzo Bernini
Spanish Steps:
Francesco De Sanctis

type
public space, monument

construction
Fontana della Barcaccia: 1629
Spanish Steps: 1725

05. Hertziana Library – Max Planck Institute For Art History

via Gregoriana 30
00187 Roma

Mon - Fri / 9.30 am - 8 pm

+ 39 06 69377739
tessera@biblhertz.it
www.biblhertz.it

A > Spagna

This library was designed following a competition by invitation held in 1995, won by the Spanish artist and architect Juan Navarro Baldeweg. The building houses the collection of Henriette Hertz, a German art collector after whom the library is named. A large grotesque mask entrance invites the public to visit the eight floors arranged on a trapeze-shaped lot immersed in the gardens of the Palazzo Zuccari. The innovative structural strategy began during the excavation stage. Certain remains of Lucio Licinio Lucullo's villa were discovered during the excavation work; this permitted the construction of a 3 metre high space, supported by 178 micro-piles sunk to a depth of 50 metres, around the exact position of the external walls. This structure supports the library space arranged around a light well. Book shelves line the external perimeters to provide soundproofing, while the reading tables face the interior, taking advantage of the natural light that filters through the three glass walls enclosing the light well. A single closed wall houses the large archives to the rear. With a plain simple design, an ancient Roman site was incorporated with elegance and innovation into a modern contemporary space.

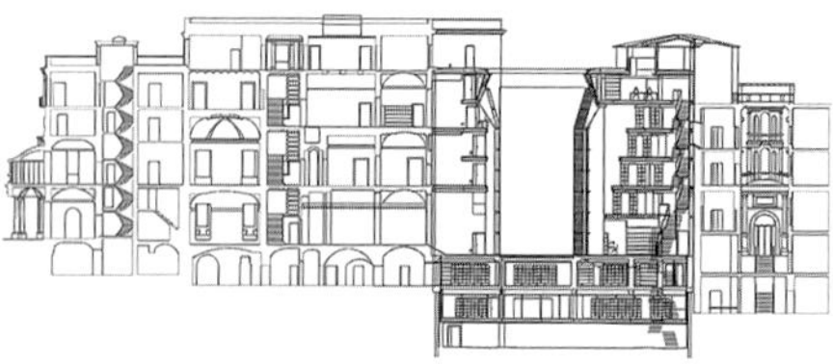

architects
Juan Navarro Baldeweg,
Da Gai Architetti

type
library

construction
2009-2012

06. Mixed Use Building

via Campania 10
00187 Roma

partially open to the public

The Mixed Use Building in via Campania designed by Studio Passarelli is one of the most famous examples of modern architecture in Rome. The building is divided into three storeys according to the purpose of the internal space: retail stores, offices spaces, and residential apartments. The entrance to the stores is recessed in behind the external glass curtain walls to create a modern version of a portico-like passage. Although initially, the glass structure seems to be in complete contrast with its context, in reality it is the element that maintains a constant dialogue with the history of its surroundings. Geometrically, it is the same height as the Aurelian Walls, and through the glass wall, it reflects the ancient materials, highlighting the links with the past, present and future. The staggered terraces of the residential layout (*raumplan*) are in deliberate contrast with the regular structure of the office block below.

89 / 490 / 495 >
C.so D'Italia / Po

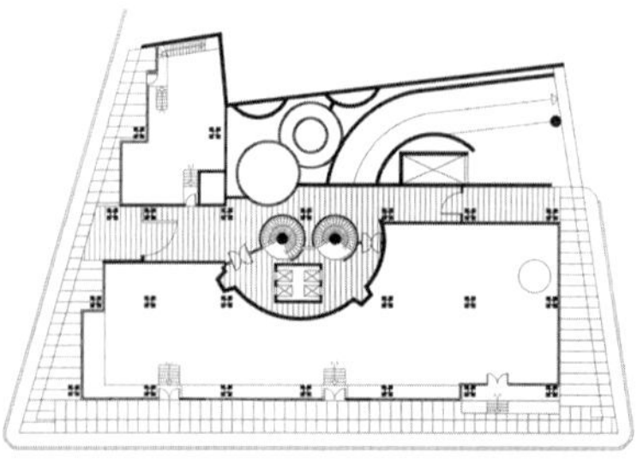

© Luca Farinelli

architects
Studio Passarelli

type
multipurpose building

construction
1964

07. Albergo degli Ambasciatori and Grand Hotel Palace

via Vittorio Veneto 62-70
00186 Roma

partially open to the public

Grand Hotel Palace:
+39 06 47871
info.rome@milleniumhotels.com
www.grandhotelpalacerome.com

52 / 53 / 61 / 63 / 83 / 160 / C3 / N1 / N4 / N25 > Veneto / Emilia

The architecture of the Albergo degli Ambasciatori, designed by Marcello Piacentini and Emilio Vogt, is highlighted by the use of white travertine and ochre yellow stone. The window openings are framed by elegant half pilasters or columns, and the crowning cornice is composed of arches that form a loggia overlooking the city. This element gives the upper part of the building a lighter effect thanks to the architect's use of rhythm and space. One of the outstanding elements of the Albergo degli Ambasciatori is the series of frescoes by the Venetian painter, Guido Candorin, that decorate the salon-restaurant, depicting the celebrities of Roman society of the period. The commission to redesign the interiors of the Albergo degli Ambasciatori, (today, the Grand Hotel Palace), was assigned to the Italo Rota architectural firm. The contemporary design is not discordant with the choices made by Piacentini and Vogt, but focuses on the most quintessential aspects, through the use of lighting and materials.

architects
Albergo degli Ambasciatori:
Marcello Piacentini,
Emilio Vogt
Grand Hotel Palace:
Italo Rota

type
hotel

construction
Albergo degli Ambasciatori:
1925-1927
Grand Hotel Palace:
2009-2010

08. Davide Cenci Store

via di Campo Marzio 1-7
00186 Roma

Mon - Sat /
10.30 am - 7.30 pm

+39 06 6990681

www.davidecenci.com

The fil rouge used by studio Alvisi Kirimoto for restyling the Davide Cenci luxury menswear store, is "a celebration of tradition". Columns and mouldings form the backdrop for this intervention that highlights tradition and focusses on revamping the brand with an innovative elegant look. Roman Botticino marble and mahogany are the materials that blend with fabric in this project: fabric that is transformed from the weave of exclusive tailoring into "contemporary draping" in the space that previously housed the cutting and tailoring room. Orange is the colour selected for the geometrical decor created with fabric-covered panels. The atmosphere in Davide Cenci Store is that of a space that is perfectly at ease with its distinguished history while being completely coherent with the present and future of high end tailoring.

119 / 628 > Corso / L.go Chigi

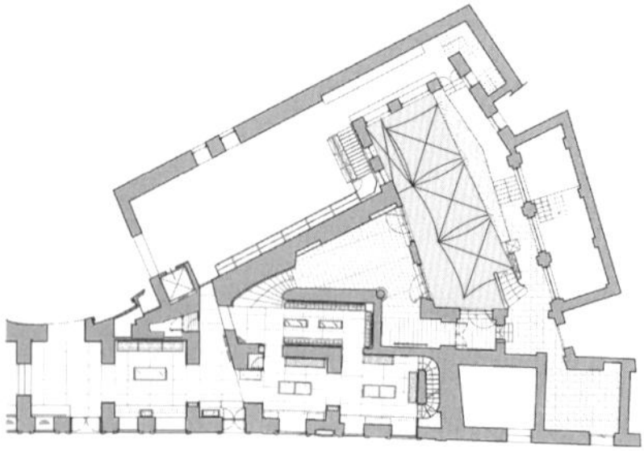

© courtesy of Alvisi Kirimoto Architects

architects	type	construction
Alvisi Kirimoto	retail	2015

09. Fountain of the Four Rivers

piazza Navona
00186 Roma

external viewing only

70 / 81 / 87 / 492 / 628 / N6 / N7 >
Senato / Rinascimento

The Fountain of the Four Rivers, created by Gian Lorenzo Bernini, and commissioned by Pope Innocent X, incorporates many of the artistic features that made the sculptor famous, like the interrelation between solids and voids, and his capacity to accentuate suspension among various elements in his compositions. The fountain symbolises the great rivers of the four continents known at that time: the Nile, the Ganges, the Danube, and the Rio de la Plata. The central element is composed of the Roman copy of an Egyptian obelisk from the Circus of Maxentius, and the great power of this work is precisely in the base of the vertical element: the void below the obelisk creates a feeling of disorientation in the viewer, that conveys even greater emotion. Concealed in the composition, we discover creatures from land and sea linked to the symbology of the rivers represented. Among the figures is the dolphin, symbol of the Pamphili family, together with the papal coat of arms. Allegory and symbology, two of the distinctive features, together with the papal coat of arms. Allegory and symbology as distinctive trait of the Roman Baroque that has had in Bernini one of the greatest exponents.

architects
Gian Lorenzo Bernini

type
monument

construction
1648-1651

10. Pantheon

piazza della Rotonda
00186 Roma

Mon - Sat /
8.30 am - 7.30 pm
Sun / 9 am - 6 pm

+39 06 68300230

www.beniculturali.it

A > Barberini

30 / 70 / 81 / 87 / 130F / 492 / 628 / C3 / N6 / N7 / N25 > Rinascimento
30 / 40 / 46 /62 / 64 / 70 / 81 / 87 / 130F / 190F / 492 / 628 / 916 / 916F / N46 / N70 / N98 / N904 / N913 > Argentina

From the ancient Greek, "place of all the gods", the Pantheon is one of the most famous pieces of architecture in the world. Currently named Santa Maria della Rotonda, it opens onto the piazza through an octastyle pronaos, but once inside the the central space, the viewer's gaze is immediately drawn upwards to the oculus inside the curve of the dome, which has become one of the symbolic elements of this famous building. With its coffered ceiling and imposing diameter, this is currently one of the largest self-supporting domes in the world. The interior of the Pantheon is divided into two orders; the first is composed of six alcoves flanked by a pair of columns, the entrance and apse alcoves opposite one another, are framed by two columns projecting from the walls. The upper order is composed of openings framed by multicoloured marble that is continued to clad the entire upper order. The Pantheon is one of the only buildings that has remained intact throughout the centuries. For this reason it is possible to perceive the layers of time within the building, lit by its "oculus dei" that illuminates this unique and amazing space.

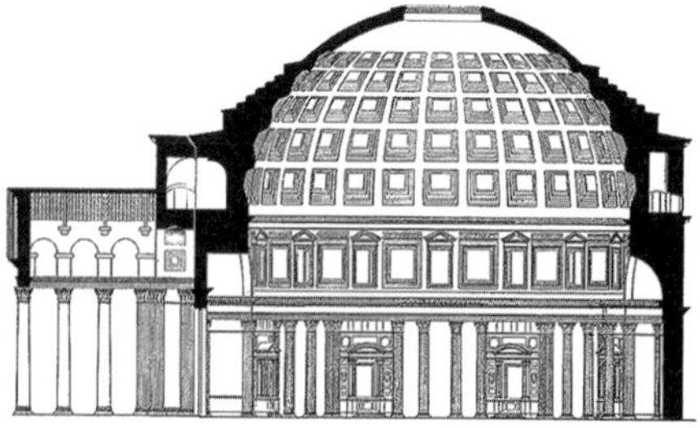

architects
-

type
monument

construction
120-124 A.D.

11. Trevi Fountain

piazza di Trevi
00186 Roma

external viewing only

+39 06 0608

www.turismoroma.it

A > Barberini

62 / 63 / 83 / 85 / 119 / 160 / 492 / C3 / N4 / N5 / N12 / N25 > Corso/Minghetti

"Oh my God!" With these words the fascinating Anita Ekberg gracefully plunged into the most famous fountain in Italy. Hidden in the midst of narrow winding streets, still today the Trevi Fountain never fails to amaze visitors like a newly discovered contemporary work of art. It was designed by Nicola Salvi 240 years ago, as part of the underground system of the Virgin aqueduct. The symbolic figure stands in a niche at the top of the fountain directing her gaze towards the original source. The sea god Neptune dominates the central section, and with two tritons, controls the Power and Impetuosity of the sea, represented by two horses, while Salubrity and Abundance, works by Filippo Valle, are positioned in the side niches. In the uppermost section, four statues represent the benefits of water in different seasons. Legend has it that the large round urn on the eastern parapet was installed to block the view of the fountain from the shop of a local barber who had criticised the fountain. Today it is a pilgrimage for visitors who toss in a coin in the hopes of returning to Rome and to the Trevi fountain. A wish shared by Mastroianni: "Come here, Marcello". "Yes Silvia, I am coming in too".

architects
Nicola Salvi,
Giuseppe Pannini

type
monument

construction
1731-1762

12. Quirinale Palace and Papal Stables Renovation

Quirinale Palace:
piazza del Quirinale
Papal Stables renovation:
via XXIV Maggio 16
00186 Roma

Quirinale Palace:
Tue - Wed, Fri - Sun /
9.30 am - 4 pm
Mon, Thu / closed
Recovery of Scuderie Papali:
Sun - Thu / 10 am - 8 pm
Fri - Sat / 10 am - 10.30 pm

Quirinale Palace:
+39 06 46991
Papal Stables renovation:
+39 02 92897722
info@scuderiequirinale.it
www.quirinale.it
www.scuderiequirinale.it

A > Repubblica

40 / 60 / 64 / 70 / 170 / H / N7 / N8 / N9 / N15 / N18 > Nazionale / Quirinale

On one of the oldest hills in Rome sits the residence of the President of the Italian Republic, and home to works by famous artists and architects. In 1722, Alessandro Specchi, who also designed the palace, began the construction of the Papal stables completed 10 years later by Ferdinando Fuga. The building is set against the wall that encloses the Colonna Gardens and is built on the remains of the temple of Serapis, parts of which have been rendered visible. The building's original function as storage remained until 1938, and only sixty years later, the palace was restored to create an exhibition space. The project, by Gae Aulenti, shows a complete integration of the contemporary with the past. The interior has been restored with extreme care, using travertine stone on the ground floor and grey oak on the other floors. The original wall structure was not changed. The walls were simply cleaned and finished with tinted lime wash recalling the traditional Roman plaster render. Plasterboard panels were used to divide up the exhibition spaces. The distance between the two sections, that form one box positioned within another, conceals all the electrical equipment. The refined detailing is enhanced further by the clever lighting effects by Piero Castiglione.

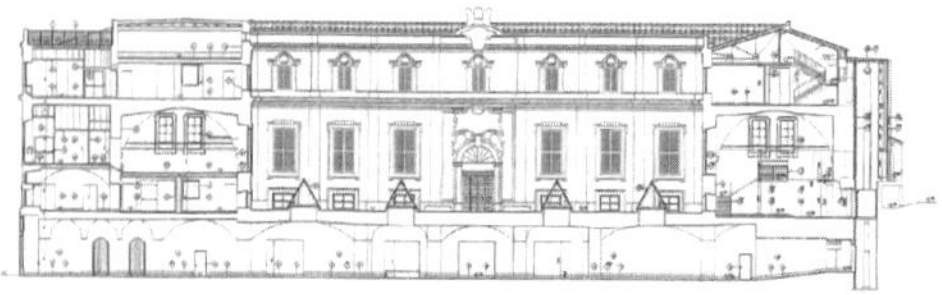

© Archivio Gae Aulenti

architects
Quirinale Palace: Ottaviano Mascherino, Gian Lorenzo Bernini, Ferdinando Fuga, Domenico Fontana
Papal Stables renovation: Gae Aulenti

type
residential, cultural centre

construction
Quirinale Palace: 1583
Papal Stables renovation: 1997-1999

13. Palazzo delle Esposizioni Restoration and Serra Piacentini Reconstruction

via Milano 9
00186 Rome

Mon / closed
Tue - Thu / 10 am - 8 pm
Fri - Sat / 10 am - 10.30 pm
Sun / 10 am - 8 pm

+39 02 39967500

www.palazzoesposizioni.it

64 / 70 / 170 / H / N7 / N8 / N9 / N15 / N18 > Nazionale/ Esposizioni

This intervention is an integrated part of the urban transformation in the area behind the modern buildings by Pio Piacentini. The innovative choices have provided clever urban integration to connect the area with via Piacenza. The new structure becomes lighter and more transparent as it rises thanks to a trilithic material concept: the base walls support the technical sections faced in travertine stone, made lighter and transparent with a glassed 'greenhouse' effect and roofing. The purity of line is enhanced by the slender structural profiles adopted for the windows, adding a luminous symbolic light effect. The glass 'greenhouse' connects with the palace and urban fabric, represented as a functional glass cube from a climatic and environmental viewpoint. The laminated, tempered structural glass also has low emissivity levels. When necessary it can be screened off by sliding curtains with high protection and reflection capacity. The minimalist design and innovative techniques have made a great contribution to the institutional and architectural value of the Palazzo delle Esposizioni.

© ABDR Architetti Associati

architects
ABDR Architetti Associati

type
cultural centre

construction
2007

14. Roma Termini Railway Station

Station: piazza del Cinquecento
Adjacent buildings:
via Marsala e via Giolitti
Mercato Centrale:
via Giovanni Giolitti 36
00186 Rome

Station and Adjacent buildings:
open to the public
Mercato Centrale:
Mon - Sun / 8 am - 12 pm

Mercato Centrale:
+39 06 46202900
info@mercatocentrale.it
marketing@mercatocentrale.it
www.romatermini.com
www.mercatocentrale.it

5 /14 > Termini

A / B > Termini

105> Termini
70 > Giolitti

Rome Central Station is the largest in Italy, originally built in the 19th century near the ancient Baths of Diocletian from where it takes its name. In 1938, Angiolo Mazzoni was commissioned to create a structure to concentrate all services to the sides of the existing train tracks. The building by Salvatore Bianchi (1869) was set back, moving the entrance to piazza dei Cinquecento, and the platforms were separated from the city by side buildings, connected by an underground level with retail stores and technical services. Pink Travertine stone, Carrara marble, wood and sand-blasted brick, create a link with the traditional and monumental nature of Rome. The front building was completed in 1951 by two competition winning groups of architects. The atrium, offices, gallery, and bar-restaurant are housed in a new rectangular structure covered by a projecting cantilever roof supported by 33 columns. The undulated roof curves vary between 9 and 13 meters in height: this design is key to its effect as a public piazza. The Cappa Mazzoniana building, that had been out of use for years, was restored and opened as a new covered central market in 2016, with the entrance in via Giolitti: 17 artisan food stores occupy the 2,000 square metres on the ground floor, a wine store/bar on the first floor, and an events area on the top floor.

© pio3 / Shutterstock.com

architects
Railway Station:
Angiolo Mazzoni / Leo Calini, Massimo Castellazzi, Vasco Fadigati, Eugenio Montuori, Achille Pintorello, Annibale Vitellozzi
Mercato Centrale: Studio Q-bic (Luca and Marco Baldini)

type
railway station

construction
Railway Station:
1938-1943 / 1948-1951
Mercato Centrale: 2016

15. Restoration of the Campo Carleo "shops" and walkways at the Trajan Markets

via IV Novembre 94
00186 Rome

Mon - Sun /
9.30 am - 7.30 pm

+39 06 0608
info@mercatiditraiano.it
www.mercatiditraiano.it

40 / 60 / 64 / 70 / 170 / H / N7 / N8 / N9 / N15 / N18 >
Nazionale/Quirinale

When they began work on the Trajan markets, Nemesi Studio e Labics developed a project design to convert the area into a permanent exhibition space dedicated to Imperial Roman architecture. The renovation of the small stores or Tabernae is the result of detailed restoration work, consolidation, conservative rehabilitation and finishes to close an access archway to protect the entrance from bad weather. The wall structure had not suffered any damage and was reinforced using innovative materials like acrylic glass for adherence panels. The traditional classic style opens onto the city with a walkway from Campo Carleo to replace the previous passageway which had always been used by visitors to view the ancient ruins. The impact of this project lies in the continuous improving of the ancient wall structure and the archaeological remains that are perfectly integrated with the contemporary elements of the intervention: lines, surfaces and materials like Corten steel and stainless steel cables integrate perfectly with the surrounding context, intensifying the effect of the ancient structure and providing perfect visibility.

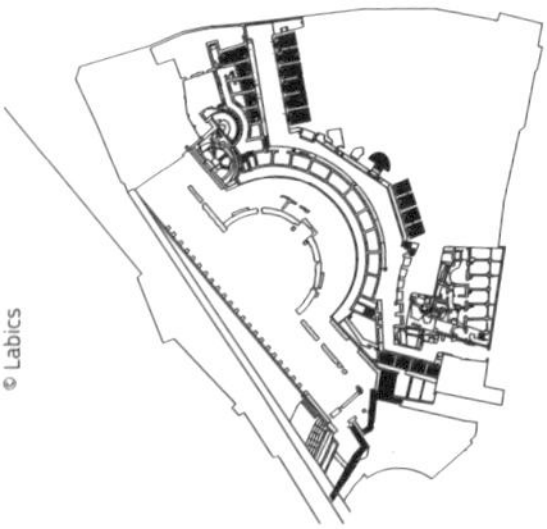

© Labics

© Marco Cappelletti

architects
Labics, Nemesi Studio

type
public space, monument

construction
1998-2004

16. Tomb of the Unknown Soldier in the Vittoriano

piazza Venezia
00186 Rome

Mon - Thu /
9.30 am - 7.30 pm
Fri - Sat / 9.30 am - 10 pm
Sun / 9.30 am - 8.30 pm

+39 06 6780664

85 / 87 / 118 > Fori Imperiali
46 / N3 > P.za Venezia

The monumental complex of "the Secular Temple of the Nation" commonly known as Altare della Patria [Altar of the Fatherland], contains the remains of an unknown soldier killed during the First World War. It was created to celebrate the heroism of millions of soldiers who had fought to defend the fatherland. Maria Bergamas, the mother of an Austrian volunteer in the Italian army chose one of the eleven unknown soldiers, who was laid in a porphyry sarcophagus, and placed in a room below a statue of the Dea Roma, accessed by a staircase that descends directly from the entrance. The crypt is composed of four pillars supporting the sculptured work, creating a space in Greek Cross form with an oval dome covered with frescoes and mosaics designed by Giulio Bargellini. The stone and marble create a solemn atmosphere and are taken from some of the First World War battlefields as a commemoration: limestone and black and white marble paving divide the various zones in the space, surrounded by a high wainscot in Karst stone and brick clad walls.

architects
Armando Brasini

type
monument

construction
1935

17. Exhibition Hall in the Roman Garden, Capitoline Museums

piazza del Campidoglio 1
00186 Rome

Mon - Sun /
9.30 am - 7.30 pm

+39 06 0608

www.museicapitolini.org

30 / 44 / 51 / 63 / 81 / 83 / 85 / 87 / 118 / 130F / 160 / 170 / 628 / 715 / 716 / 781 / 63 / H / N3 / N8 / N9 / N19 > Teatro Marcello / Ara Coeli

"An ongoing invention" was the description of the masterpiece by 80 year old architect, Carlo Aymonino, in the ancient Roman Gardens in the Capitoline Museums. Initially, the architect "did not want to touch the Campidoglio", but after intense research into the proposal and given his passion for sculpture, he agreed to intervene. The Capitoline Museums have been extended by 3,000 square metres to enclose the exedra of Marcus Aurelius: Aymonino honoured the emperor with a new home built of steel and glass, flooding the interior with natural light. Among remains of foundations of the Temple of Jupiter Capitolinus and other recently discovered archaeological finds in the garden, the bronze statue stands on a pedestal 1.5 metres high, on the right-hand side of the hall created to roof the gardens. It has an elliptical layout like the piazza by Michelangelo and is 8 metres high, with white walls, glass panels, and Venetian stone and mortar flooring. Thick pillars alternate with slender steel columns to support the roof, originally designed with triangular glass sections, but later changed to square coffered panels set in a modular steel structure.

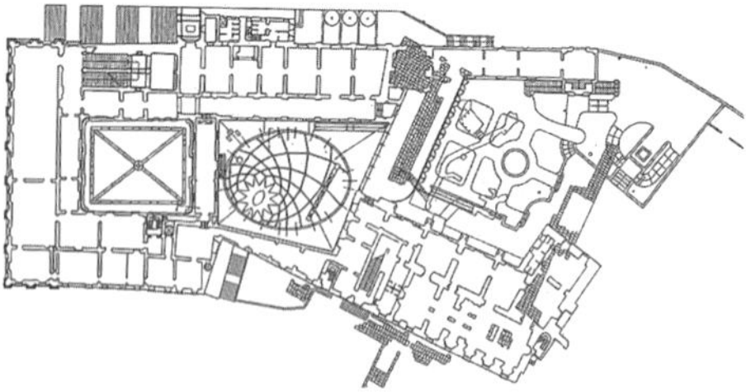

architects	type	construction
Carlo Aymonino	cultural centre	1993-2005

18. Roman Forum

via della Salara Vecchia 5/6
00186 Rome

Mon - Sun / 9 am - 7 pm

+39 06 0608

www.turismoroma.it

B / B1 > Colosseo

85 / 87 / 118 >
Fori Imperiali

A famous example of architectural stratification, the monuments of the Forum have been subject to layers of rebuilding over the course of time, becoming one of the most important archaeological sites in Europe. The basilicas and temples are positioned along the lengthwise sides of the open rectangular space, surrounded by iron railings, while the Rostra and Arch of Septimius Severus are built on one of the shorter sides opposite the great Temple of Venus and Roma. The remains of public and religious buildings show the use of traditional constructive and design techniques. Along the via Sacra, the Curia Iulia is easily recognisable for its *opus sectile* facing, followed by the Basilica Emilia, whose remains reveal the presence of a large central nave and two narrower side aisles. At the end of the route is the Arch of Septimius Severus, 23 metres high and almost intact, while to the side, there are visible traces of the mooring pin holes on the Rostra podiums, used to attach the ships' rams. Unusual for their intact condition, are the eight columns which are all that remain of the Temple of Saturn, one of the most ancient in Rome. The design, colour, marble, stone and brick are still able to tell the story of an ancient people in today's Republican era.

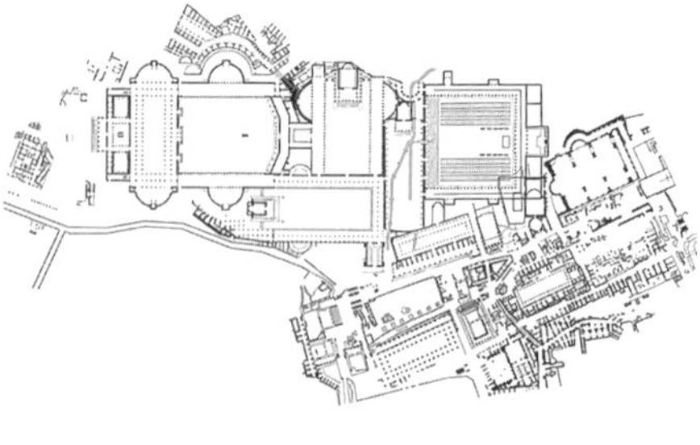

architects
-

type
archaeological park

construction
from X-VII sec. B.C.

19. Colosseum

piazza del Colosseo
00186 Rome

Mon - Sun / 8.30 am - 7 pm

+39 06 39967700
info@il-colosseo.it
www.il-colosseo.it

3 / 8 > Colosseo

B / B1 > Colosseo

51 / 75 / 85 / 87 / N2 > Colosseo
75 / 85 / 87 / 118 / C3 / N2 / N10 > Celio Vibenna

The Flavian Amphitheatre is the symbol of the Eternal City, constructed as a space for public entertainment. Built in the Domus Aurea site, near its artificial lake, it was constructed using 100,000 cubic metres of travertine stone excavated from the Tivoli quarries. It is oval in shape with an external length of 188 metres, 156 metres wide, and 58 metres high. The external facade is 4 storeys high. The first three floors are designed in classical order: numbered arches (80) are supported by Tuscan order half-columns on the first level, Ionic order on the second level, and Corinthian on the last level. The fourth level, known as the attic, is enhanced with pilasters aligned with the lower columns, and which mark the openings for the mast corbels that supported the awning or velarium. Spectators were seated in a cavea with marble tiered seating divided into 5 sections according to social status and profession. The wooden flooring of the arena, partially reconstructed today, reveals underground galleries and corridors used before great events. Today, part of the arena floor is open to the sky because of an earthquake in 1349. The Amphitheatre is undergoing substantial restoration interventions because "as long as the Coliseum exists, Rome will exist."

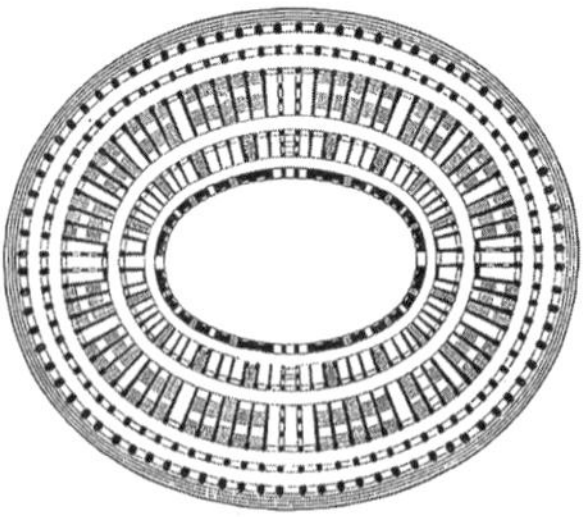

© Luca Farinelli

architects
-

type
monument

construction
72 A.D.

20. Extension to the Pius IX Library at the Pontifical Lateran University

piazza di San Giovanni Laterano 4
00186 Rome

Mon - Fri / 7 am - 7 pm
Sat - Sun / closed

+39 06 69895599
comunicazione@pul.it
www.pul.it

A / C > San Giovanni

81 / 792 > P.zza San Giovanni in Laterano

"To make a place for reading and text consultation as the central focus of the university". This was the principle aim of the Pontifical Lateran University in deciding to expand their library. The project was designed to preserve the books from external conditions. Originally located in the existing building, the reading room and archives have been transferred to a new building adjoining the university, accessible from the first floor. 70.000 volumes and 750 publications are stored in the six storey archive tower. The new structure is in perfect alignment with the existing building and faced with the same brickwork. Slashed openings in the facade provide plays of light and shadow, giving rhythm to the altimetric profile of the structure. They provide glimpses of the internal spaces in mahogany and white render, where the three ramped levels make up the reading room, provide work stations, and form a central courtyard. The courtyard gives a view of the foyer on the ground floor which houses the practical and technical elements: lockers, computers, a professors' reading room and the librarians' work stations. In 2009, the project won the IN/ARCH-ANCE 2009 national architectural award.

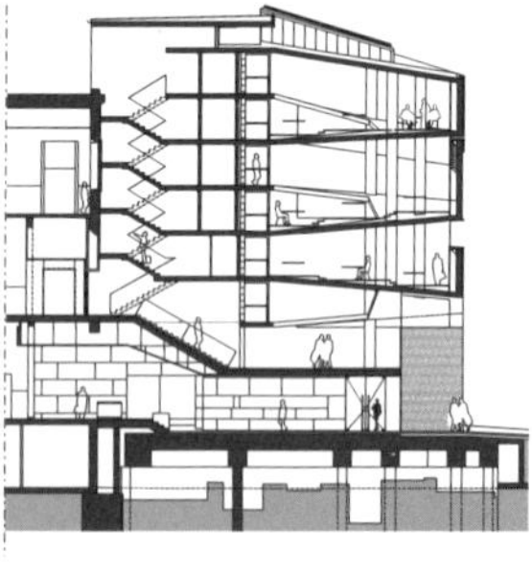

© King Roselli Architetti Associati

architects
King Roselli Architetti Associati

type
library

construction
2003-2016

21. Rhinoceros Palace. Fondazione Alda Fendi-Esperimenti

via dei Cerchi 21
00186 Rome

Mon - Sun / 10 am - 10 pm

+39 340 6430435
info@fondazionealdafendi-esperimenti.it
www.fondazionealdafendi-esperimenti.it

B / B1 > Colosseo

51 / 81 / 85 / 87 / 118 / 160 / 628 / 715 / C3
> Cerchi / Bocca della Verità

The Rhinoceros Palace was conceived by Alda Fendi and Raffaele Curi to provide a multi-use exhibition space, 24 residential apartments, retail stores and a restaurant-bar that offers panoramic views of the city. The conservation of the building's facade, coherent with the surrounding context, was executed together with the restoration project that included innovative logistics systems, kitchen and bathroom interiors, window framing and furnishings. Stainless steel panels sit alongside ancient walls, and metal railing structures enhance centuries-old staircases. The Alda Fendi-Esperimenti foundation occupies 3,500 square metres spread over six floors, designed as exhibition spaces. Only the first two floors are formally recognised as staging areas. The project was completed on schedule despite the complex redevelopment process, and today the building is recognised as a masterpiece of architecture, town planning, and above all, art. The building had the honour of showing for the first time in Italy, Michelangelo's *Crouching Boy*, on loan from the Hermitage Museum in St. Petersburg.

architects
Ateliers Jean Nouvel

type
multipurpose building

construction
2012-2018

22. Roma Ostiense Post Office Building

via Marmorata 4
00153 Rome

Mon - Fri / 8.30 am - 6 pm
Sat / 8.30 am - 1 pm
Sun / closed

+39 06 57018228

3 > Marmorata
8 > Galvani

B / B1 > Piramide

23 / 75 / 280 / 716 / N3 / N9 / N10 > Marmorata Galvani

In the 1930s it became necessary to extend public services to the city limits, and in 1932, a competition was launched to design four new post office buildings. The Roma Ostiense Post Office building in via Marmorata is part of a functional town planning development scheme that included viale Mazzini, via Taranto and piazza Bologna. This building shows architectural rationalism in its maximum experimental expression, where the Golden Ratio and geometrical relations form the basis of the project design. Wide, regular steps lead to the monumental entrance, with its glazed portico in close contact with the city. Light floods through an oval skylight accentuating the modern architectural elements. The main facade is composed of a perfectly geometrical grid design in marble, with square openings that underline the functional internal spaces. The facades of the two projecting side wings feature a lattice composition to accentuate the line of the internal stairways.

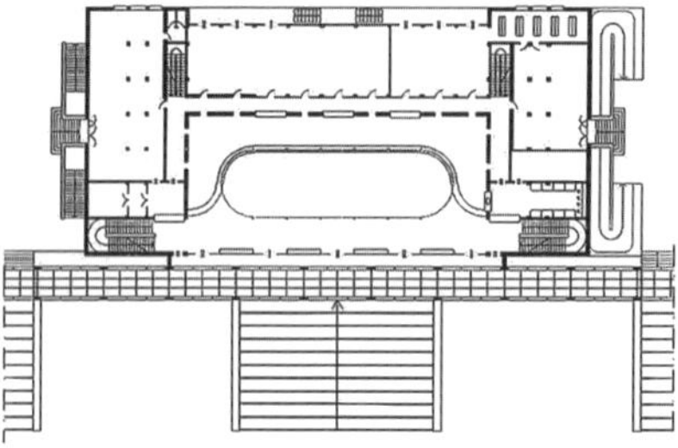

architects
Mario De Renzi,
Adalberto Libera

type
offices

construction
1933-1935 / 1966-1968 /
1998-1999

23. Ex-Testaccio Slaughterhouse Restoration

largo Giovanni Battista Marzi 10, piazza Orazio Giustiniani 4
00186 Rome

Tue - Sun / 2 pm - 8 pm
Mon / closed

+39 06 39967500
info.mattatoio@palaexpo.it
www.mattatoioroma.it

B / B1 > Piramide

719 > Franklin

The cultural hub in the ex-industrial complex by Gioacchino Ersoch (1880) was created following a Programme Agreement between Università Roma Tre and the Rome City Council. The Roman architectural firm, Insula, was responsible for the faithful restoration and conservative renovation of the tuff stone and brick facades and the new teaching and cultural space layouts. As well as demolishing all the superfluous added elements and extensions to internal spaces, the architects and engineers designed the project for Pavilion 2B destined for the Faculty of Architecture. The harmonious interior design divides the internal space using mobile partitions that echo the position of the previous livestock holding pens, in a total area of 840 square metres. The six walls are aligned between pairs of iron Polonceau trusses that enhance the ceiling; the partitions are composed of permanent steel and glass sections, with opaque folding panels that are used to divide and adapt the internal space between 120 and 720 square metres, according to necessity.

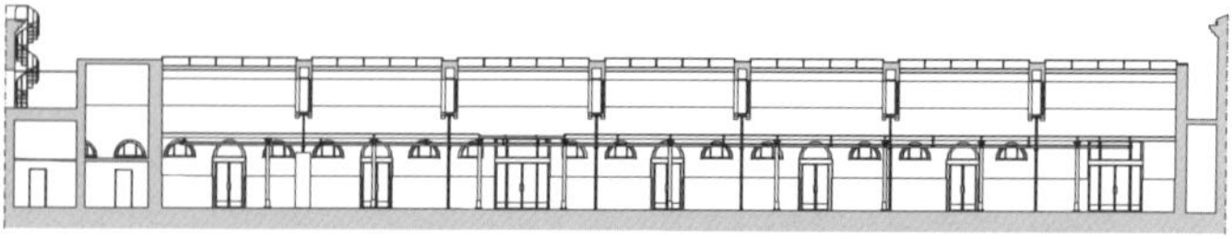

architects
Insula architettura
e ingegneria

type
cultural centre

construction
2008-2013

24. Casa della Gioventù in Trastevere

largo Ascianghi 5
00186 Rome

external viewing only

3 / 8 > Trastevere / Min. P. Istruzione

8BUS > Trastevere / Min. P. Istruzione

This iconic design by Luigi Moretti, is renowned for its architecture, its position in the urban fabric, and the visual communication between its internal public spaces. The functional concept was defined by three entrances; the complex was divided into three geometrical blocks with distinct functions, in answer to the propaganda of the period. The via Ascianghi entrance led to the health centre, via Induno housed the sports and recreation centre, and the main entrance from the piazza, led to the administrative and organisational offices, housed in the Torre Littoria, aligned with an internal spiral staircase. The combination of traditional classic design and modern rational architecture had a strong impact on the internal and external composition. The complex was built of reinforced concrete with travertine stone cladding. The interior flooring was covered in Imperial grey and Amiata red linoleum. A multi-use gym, and another for boxing and fencing were superimposed, as can be seen by the wall murals showing sports activities. The other educational areas were spacious and flexible, with glazed curtain walls. Some parts are not accessible as the building is currently under restoration.

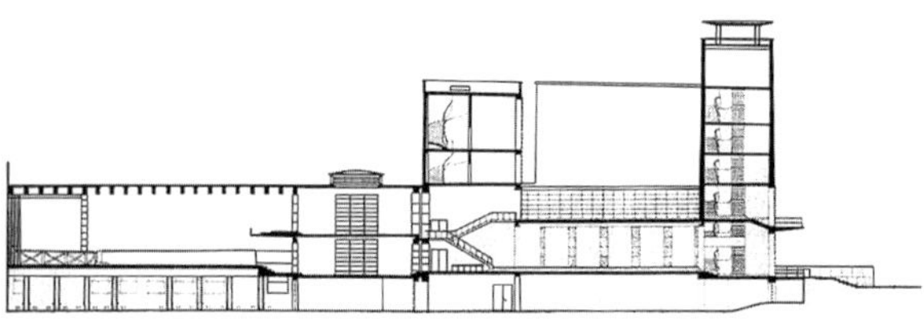

© Luca Farinelli

architects
Luigi Moretti

type
exhibition space

construction
1933-1936

25. Tempietto of San Pietro in Montorio

piazza di S. Pietro in Montorio 3
00186 Rome

Mon - Sat / 8.30 am - 12 am, 3 pm - 4 pm
Sun / 8.30 am - 12 am

+39 06 5813940
sanpietroinmontorio@libero.it
www.sanpietroinmontorio.it

115 > Garibaldi/ Iacobucci

The small temple of San Pietro in Montorio is located in the monastery of the same name, supposed location of St. Peter's martyrdom. The centre floor plan and the geometrical proportions of the various elements are typical of those in the first centuries of Roman Renaissance architecture. Its monumental elegance can be seen in the 5 circular steps that surround the whole building, and the 16 Tuscan columns in grey granite that form the entrance portico to the cella. The floor is paved in multi-coloured marble, and measures 4.5 metres in diameter. Four minor, and four major niches are carved into the walls to house the statues of the Evangelists. On the upper level, a drum whose height is equal to the radius, is decorated with pilasters aligned with the columns beneath. They support the semi-spherical dome in reinforced concrete completed by a roof lantern. It is said that the original plan was to include 16 pilasters inside to correspond with the external columns, and those planned for the cloister. However, because of lack of space, Bramante decided to indicate the link with the columns using a different intercolumniation, in order to position the entrance correctly.

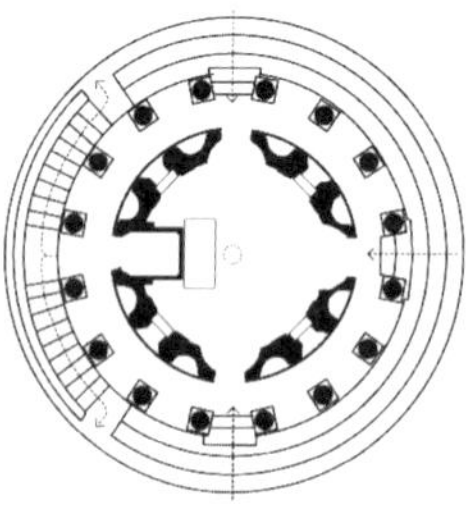

architects
Donato Bramante

type
monument

construction
1510

26. Castel Sant'Angelo

lungotevere Castello 50
00186 Rome

Mon - Sun / 9 am - 7.30 pm

+39 06 6819111
+39 06 39967600
pm-laz@beniculturali.it
www.castelsantangelo.beniculturali.it

A > Ottaviano

23 / 34 / 40 / 49 / 87 / 280 / 492 / 926 7 982 / 990 > Borgo Sant'angelo

Castel Sant'Angelo is a structure where past and present are inextricably linked, where functions may change, but the form remains. Its current form is the result of reconstruction during the Middle Ages and Renaissance, transforming it into a fortress, prison, papal refuge, military barracks, and palace for festivities. Built as a mausoleum for the Emperor Hadrian, today it is a national museum, under the direction of MIBAC, and is composed of stratified geometrical layers. The ancient mausoleum has a square base, 89 metres per side, and is 15 metres high. A 20 metre high cylindrical structure is built above, forming a landmark on the skyline along the Tiber. A small circular temple 20 metres high, surrounded by columns, is topped by a statue of St. Michael archangel, symbol of the end of the plague. A spiral staircase leads to Hadrian's funeral chamber, courtyards, rooms, apartments and loggias, decorated and frescoed with ancient painting techniques. The Castello is connected to the Vatican State by a fortified elevated corridor called the "passetto", built by Clement VII as a secret passage though the Leonine Wall, while the Ponte Elio connects the Castello with the Campo Marzio.

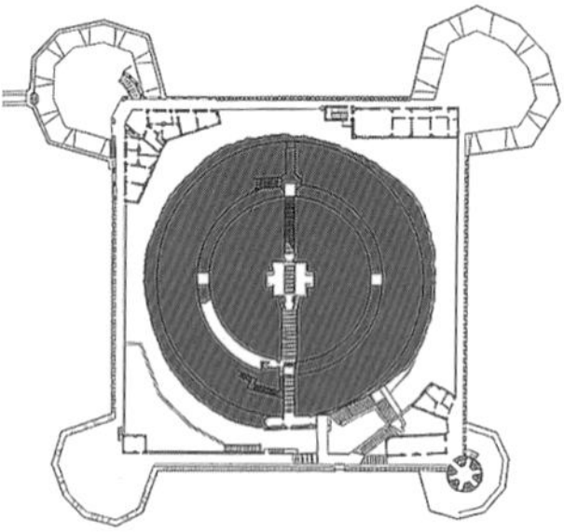

architects
-

type
monument

construction
130-139 A.D. / 1447-1527

27. Via della Conciliazione

via della Conciliazione
00186 Rome

open to the public

A > Ottaviano

40 > Borgo Sant'angelo

Via della Conciliazione, the famous street that leads from the city centre up to St. Peter's Basilica, represents one of the great modern works of urbanisation. Its construction, followed by the Lateran Treaties, marked the figurative passage of Rome as the capital of the Papal state to that of capital of the State of Italy, and recalls the demolition of the "Spina dei Borghi", ordered by Mussolini for the redevelopment of the entire city block. Marcello Piacentini and Attilio Spaccarelli were in charge of the reconstruction in Neoclassical style, of Borgo, one of the historical areas of the city. In October 28th, 1936, the Duce gave the first symbolic blow with a pickaxe, and in 1950 the street was completed with the installation of 28 obelisks along both sides, that now light up the whole area at night. The Renaissance palaces designed by Bramante, Peruzzi and Maderno, including Palazzo Convertendi and Palazzo Rusticucci, were demolished and rebuilt using the same materials in a new form, aligned with the gardens of Castel Sant'Angelo. Very few monuments remained intact, along with decorative detailing on other palaces, churches and fountains.

architects
Marcello Piacentini,
Attilio Spaccarelli

type
infrastructure

construction
1936

28. St. Peter's Basilica

piazza San Pietro
00186 Rome

Summer: Mon - Sun /
7 am - 7 pm
Winter: Mon - Sun /
7 am - 6.30 pm

+39 06 69883731
+39 06 69883462
+39 06 69883731
www.vatican.va

19 > Risorgimento / San Pietro

A > Ottaviano

49 > Viale Vaticano
23 / 982 / n3s > Risorgimento / Porta Angelica
34 / 46 / 98 / 190F / 881 / 916 / 916F / 982 / n46 / n98 / n904 > Cavallegeri / S. Pietro

St. Peter's is the symbol of the Vatican State and an icon in the history of Christendom. It was built on the ruins of a Constantinian basilica from the 4th century: an elongated structure with five naves. Rossellino was the first to intervene by adding a choir stall, completed by Bramante, whose project for the church revolutionised the original design, with a Greek cross layout and a dome supported on four large pillars, that became the fundamental elements for the basilica. In the debate to decide between a Greek or Latin cross design, Antonio da Sangallo il Giovane united the two, and added two bell towers. After his death, Michelangelo chose the Greek cross layout, designing the internal space, and adding a pronaos; he also designed the portico and attic to provide a uniform facade. After 1605, Carlo Maderno completed the work with a further three bays, chapels recessed into the deep perimeter walls at the sides of the lateral naves, under oval domes like small roof lanterns. The facade was enhanced with two bell towers with niches, and a crowning element with roof lantern. Several structural problems were resolved by Gian Lorenzo Bernini, who also designed the famous St. Peter's square.

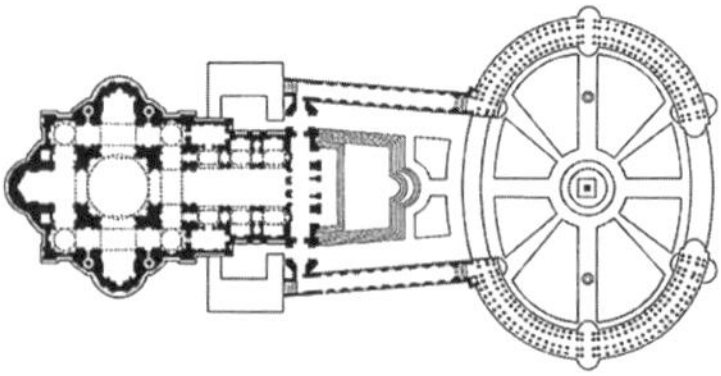

architects
Bernardo Rossellino / Donato Bramante / Antonio da Sangallo il Giovane / Raffaello, Giuliano da Sangallo, Fra' Giocondo / Michelangelo / Carlo Maderno

type
church

construction
1506-1626

29. New Wing of the Vatican Museums

viale Vaticano
00186 Rome

Mon - Sat / 9 am - 6 pm
Last Sunday of each month / 9 am - 2 pm

+39 06 69884676
+39 06 69883145
info.mv@scv.va
www.museivaticani.va/content/museivaticani/it.

A > Ottaviano

49 > Viale Vaticano / Pisani

During Jubilee year, the Holy See decided to reorganise certain museum areas to make them more pleasant and more easily accessible to the public. The old entrances were combined to form a single exit, while the entrance was moved to one side to create a more practical and fluid route. Working with the surrounding site, different levels were constructed and united by a magnificent helical staircase 165 metres long, which led to the redistribution of the internal spaces. The ground floor houses information services and a bookshop, the ticket office is on the intermediate floor, and the top floor contains the exhibition spaces connected with the Cortile delle Corazze, which has been covered with a steel and glass roof, and from where the public can admire the St. Peter's Dome. From here, visitors can reach the other cultural spaces: the Pinacoteca, Archaeological, Ethnological and Classical Museum, and then, the long corridors leading to the Sistine Chapel.

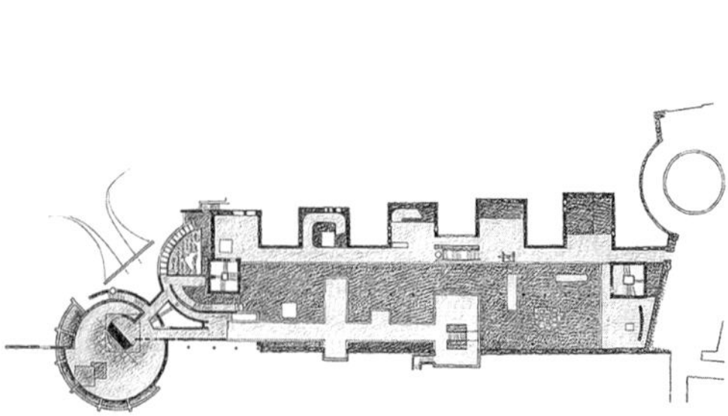

architects
Studio Passarelli

type
museum

construction
1996-2000

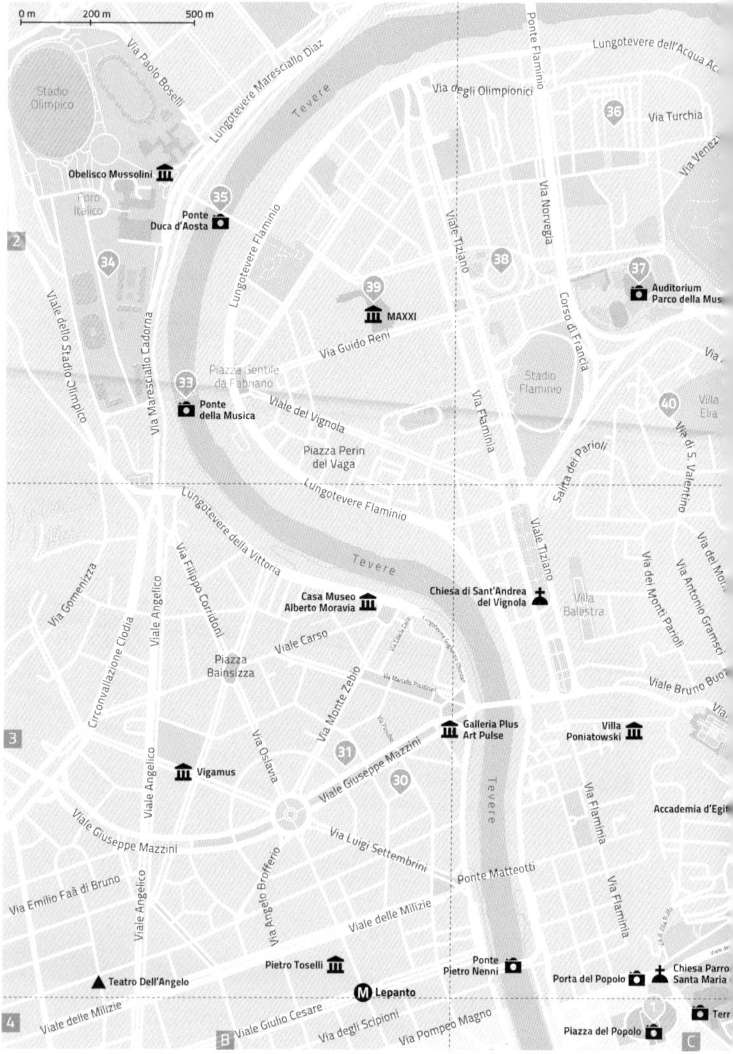
0 m
200 m
500 m
Stadio Olimpico
Via Paolo Boselli
Lungotevere Maresciallo Diaz
Tevere
Via degli Olimpionici
Ponte Flaminio
Lungotevere dell'Acqua Ac
Via Turchia
Via Venezi
Obelisco Mussolini
Foro Italico
Ponte Duca d'Aosta
Lungotevere Flaminio
Viale Tiziano
Via Norvegia
MAXXI
Auditorium Parco della Mus
Corso di Francia
Viale dello Stadio Olimpico
Via Maresciallo Cadorna
Via Guido Reni
Piazza Gentile da Fabriano
Stadio Flaminio
Ponte della Musica
Viale del Vignola
Via Flaminia
Villa Elia
Piazza Perin del Vaga
Salita dei Parioli
Via di S. Valentino
Lungotevere Flaminio
Lungotevere della Vittoria
Via Filippo Corridoni
Tevere
Viale Tiziano
Via dei Monti Parioli
Via Antonio Gramsci
Via Gomenizza
Viale Angelico
Casa Museo Alberto Moravia
Chiesa di Sant'Andrea del Vignola
Villa Balestra
Circonvallazione Clodia
Viale Carso
Piazza Bainsizza
Via Monte Zebio
Viale Bruno Buo
Via Oslavia
Galleria Plus Art Pulse
Villa Poniatowski
Vigamus
Viale Giuseppe Mazzini
Viale Angelico
Tevere
Accademia d'Egi
Via Flaminia
Viale Giuseppe Mazzini
Via Luigi Settembrini
Ponte Matteotti
Via Emilio Faà di Bruno
Via Angelo Brofferio
Viale Angelico
Viale delle Milizie
Via Flaminia
Pietro Toselli
Ponte Pietro Nenni
Porta del Popolo
Chiesa Parro Santa Maria
Teatro Dell'Angelo
Lepanto
Viale delle Milizie
Viale Giulio Cesare
Via degli Scipioni
Via Pompeo Magno
Piazza del Popolo
Terr
2
3
4
B
C
33
34
35
36
37
38
39
40
30
31

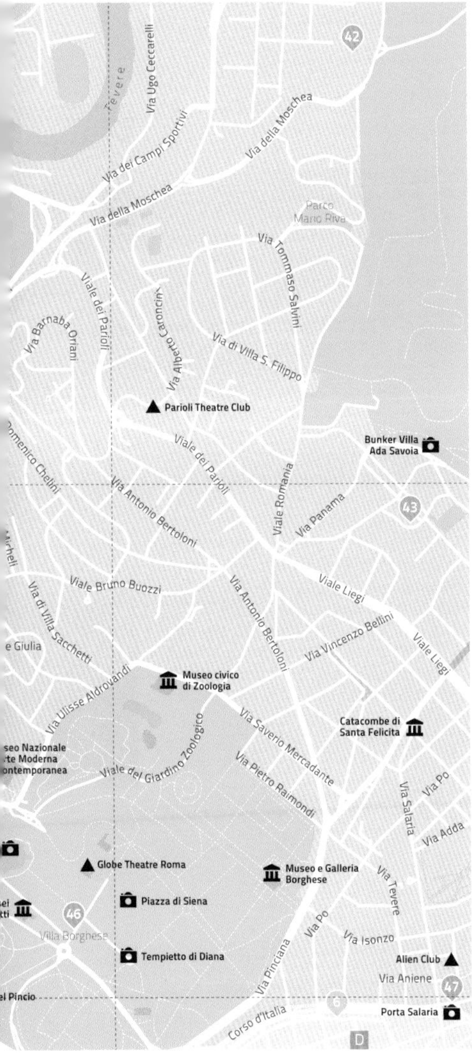

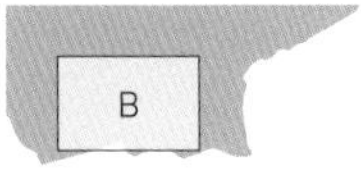

North Rome

30. Apartment Building in via Nicotera
31. Basilica del Sacro Cuore di Cristo Re
32. San Maurizio Apartment Building
33. Ponte della Musica
34. Foro Italico and Fencing Academy
35. Ponte Duca d'Aosta
36. Olympic Village
37. Parco della Musica: Auditorium and Museo Aristaios
38. Olympic Sports Arena
39. MAXXI
40. Apartment Building in via San Valentino
41. Basilica del Sacro Cuore Immacolato di Maria
42. Mosque and Islamic Cultural Centre
43. La Nave Apartment Building
44. Il Girasole Apartment Building
45. Egyptian Academy Redevelopment and Restoration
46. Villa Borghese. Gallery and Underground Parking
47. La Rinascente in piazza Fiume
48. MACRO
49. Annibaliano B1 Metro Station
50. Jonio B1 Metro Station
51. Restoration of Villa Blanc
52. Papanice House
53. Zaccardi Apartment Building

30. Apartment Building in via Nicotera

via Giovanni Nicotera 31
00195 Rome

external viewing only

495 / 628 > Montanelli

The organic form of this building's architectural design is immediately obvious. On the corner of via Nicotera and via Montanelli, it blends with the surrounding vegetation integrating with the general composition. Venturino Ventura is renowned for the expressionist aspect of his works and for the indoor-outdoor links created by the connection with the natural landscape. The continuous flower planters emphasise the linear design of the balconies in stark contrast with the three large projecting circular terraces overlooking the corner of the plot. These dominating structural elements extend towards the surrounding pine trees, almost as though supported by the branches; however, there is no bracing from below and the structures are suspended in the air and closely integrated with nature. The glass sections of the facades are hidden by plants, which also conceal the strictly regular interior layout. The intimate nature of the interior is emphasised with the use of wooden cladding on the balcony exteriors, while the elements facing the landscape, like the entrance drive, flower planters, and circular terraces, are made of exposed concrete decorated with river pebbles.

architects
Venturino Ventura

type
residential

construction
1960

31. Basilica del Sacro Cuore di Cristo Re

viale Giuseppe Mazzini 32
00195 Rome

Mon - Sun / 7 am - 8 pm

+39 06 322 3383
cristoreroma@gmail.com
www.cristoreroma.it

495 / 628 > Mazzini/ Monte Grappa

The Basilica del Sacro Cuore di Cristo Re is a symbol of Roman rationalist and religious architecture. Several schemes were proposed before the project was assigned, with Ezio and Achille Panni in charge of the engineering consulting. The pure simple lines of the church are based on a hybrid floor plan system: a Latin cross design is laid within a Greek cross layout in perfect symmetry. The interior of the high segmental arch dome with its 23 metre diameter, is completely covered with frescoes, plus a circular drum sustained by buttresses topped with statues. A staircase in white Tivoli travertine stone leads to the entrance facade that encloses the triple nave and is flanked by two slightly recessed bell towers.
The three entrance portals are surmounted by splayed arches that frame the high relief panels by Arturo Martini. The centre sculpture showing Christ the King is in a direct line with the fresco on the same theme at the end of the centre nave, 70 metres long. The strong external walls built in hand-made Roman brick, laid in double and triple rows, give an idea of the transcendent interior of the building. The colours of the apse end of the transept contrast with the grey of the smooth wall finish, above the 2 metres travertine strip around the perimeter.

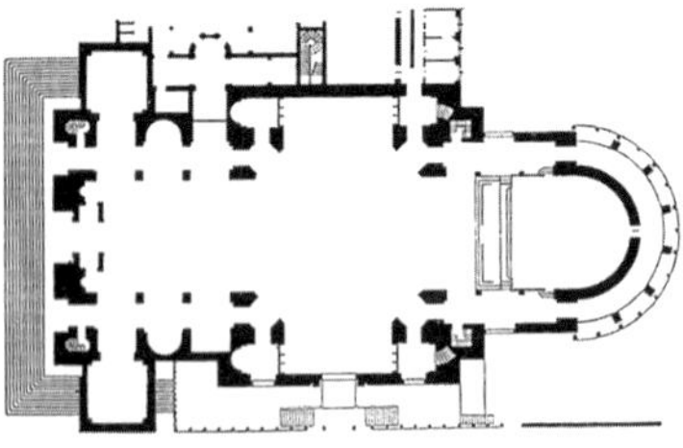

architects
Marcello Piacentini

type
church

construction
1931-1934

32. San Maurizio Apartment Building

via Romeo Romei 35-39
00136 Rome

external viewing only

69 / 495 / 89 > Clodio

"The feeling of a need for violent expansion from inside the structure towards the exterior". This was Luigi Moretti's original idea behind the design for the Palazzina San Maurizio, on the slopes of Monte Mario. Research into the work of Bernini and Borromini inspired the formal design of the exterior. In the centre of the building, composed of seven storeys plus attic floor, a large staircase and elevator lead to two luxurious apartments on each floor, with double entrances, where useful service areas frame the rectangular layout. In contrast with the rational style of the facade the projecting rounded balconies differ on each floor and do not overlap, producing at clever play of light and shadow. The refined white plaster mouldings with a granular effect reflect even greater luminosity. There are no sharp or perfectly regular corners: recessed in relation to traditional structural closure, the building is open to the exterior with projecting balconies wrapping around the structure with pure elegant lines. Despite the building's strong impact it is perceived as harmoniously integrated in the landscape and surrounding vegetation.

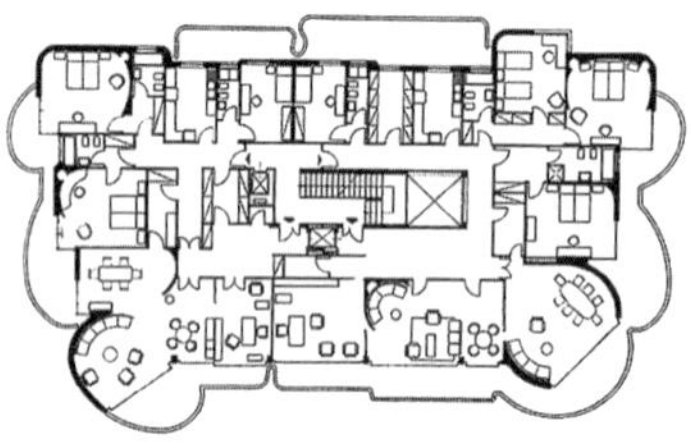

architects
Luigi Moretti

type
residential

construction
1965

33. Ponte della Musica

lungotevere Maresciallo
00195 Rome

open to the public

This bridge connects two areas of the city uniting both the contemporary with the modern. During the renovation of the Flaminio quarter, the Ponte della Musica (Music Bridge) was designed as an elegant structure suspended over the Tiber in a combination of harmoniously blended materials. The steel arches, 190 metres long and 22 metres wide in the central section, lower down, and sloping outwards from the vertical plane, are set in a platform of reinforced concrete that includes wooden cycling and walking paths on each side of the centre roadway. The arch load is supported on the banks of the Tiber where the ends of the arches are inserted, providing a further connecting element between the bridge's traffic surface and the river banks, equipped for sporting activities. Other technical systems have provided full access for pedestrians, bicycles, cars and perhaps later, also buses and trams. The infrastructure is a clear example of a perfect combination of innovative engineering, using new structural techniques and contemporary design conceived for the modern surrounding environment. In this way, the intermodal hub represents an "urban space" suspended over a natural landscape to connect it with the constructed areas.

32 / 69 / 280 / 301 / 628 / G30 / G70 > Lgt Cadorda / M.II Giardino

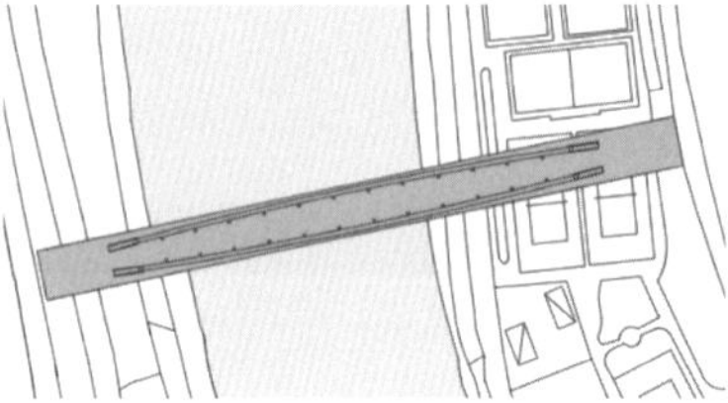

architects
Buro Happold, Davood Liaghat, Kit Powell-Williams Architects

type
bridge

construction
2008-2011

34. Foro Italico and Fencing Academy

Foro Italico:
viale del Foro Italico
Fencing Academy:
via dei Gladiatori 4
00135 Rome

external viewing only

The distribution of the space and its buildings at the Foro Italico reflect the design of the ancient Gymnasium interpreted in modern style. Every sports facility is extremely functional, and avoids any excessive formal or scenographic classical effects. Located on the slopes of Monte Mario, the main entrance facing the Ponte Duca d'Aosta, is on the north east side, while the Fencing Academy is on the southern side. The academy is composed of two buildings, a library and a weapons room, which are different in height and positioned at right-angles to each other. Two raised partitions form a walkway to connect the two spaces, underlining the proportional relationships of the building. The facades of the two blocks are perfectly uniform: the walls are clad in Carrara marble slabs giving a monolithic effect. The composition of the different rooms varies according to the layout. In the internal courtyard, the weapons room wall is completely glazed, while the library has long windows at ground level. The design of the facade along the street is in complete contrast: the weapons room is opaque and the library windows are positioned at a higher level. Despite the extensive damage to the building and Moretti's design, the structures remain an example of radical historical and architectural complexity but with rational, elegant, and sober design.

32 / 69 / 280 / 301 / 628 > Lgt Cadorna / Ostello Gioventù

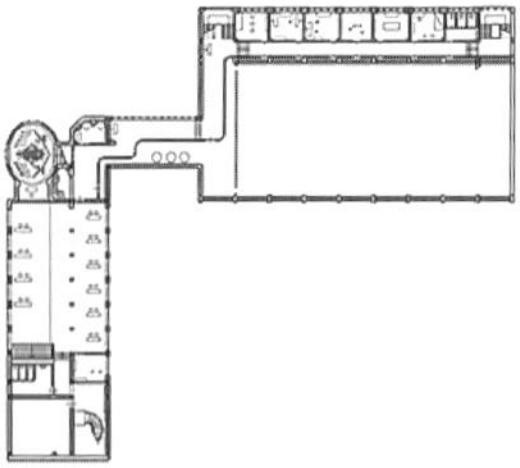

architects
Foro Italico: Enrico del Debbio, Luigi Moretti
Fencing Academy:
Luigi Moretti

type
sport complex

construction
Foro Italico: 1928-1941
Fencing Academy:
1933-1937

35. Ponte Duca d'Aosta

Ponte Duca d'Aosta
00195 Rome

open to the public

32 / 69 / 280 / 301 / 628 > De Bosis / Stadio Tennis

The Ponte Duca d'Aosta, named after Prince Emanuele Filiberto, lies in a direct line with the Mussolini obelisk, another symbol of the Foro Italico. Designed by Vincenzo Fasolo, the bridge was commissioned following a competition for contracts among the most famous Italian architects and engineers of the 1930s. Form-works, 5.2 metres high, set on reinforced concrete piles, form the foundation of this infrastructure which is striking for its single low rounded arch set over the river bed, while the other two arches are positioned on the river bends, for use in case of flooding. The structure is slender and elegant in design, even though the calculations would seem to disagree: the central arch is 100 metres long with a 30-metre section in the centre. Together with the other arches, the length of the bridge totals approximately 220.30 metres. The reinforced concrete structure is clad in Tivoli travertine stone, decorated with bas-relief sculptures depicting the battle of the Third Army on the Isonzo River. Elegant staircases lead down to the river bank level.

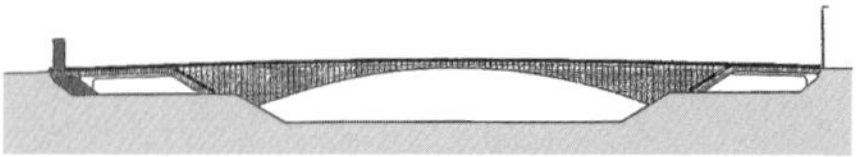

architects
Vincenzo Fasolo

type
bridge

construction
1935 1939

36. Olympic Village

Straight line buildings:
via Portogallo
Cross-shaped buildings:
via Turchia, via india,
via degli Olimpionici
00196 Rome

external viewing only

2 > Tiziano / XVII Olimpiade

201 / 223 / C3 > C.so Francia / Uruguay

The Olympic Village model project, now forms several INCIS residential buildings. A 350,000 square metres area contains 1,348 apartments covering a total of 70,000 square metres, connected by gardens rich in sculptures. The layout is based on the Roman cardi and decumani system, and buildings are arranged in plots of different shapes and heights in the terrain, coherent with modern design.
With perfect proportions between solid and void, raised blocks on columns leave open areas and service facilities available at ground level. The straight line blocks in via Bulgaria are aligned with the roadway system. The 3 to 4 storey buildings contain 14 apartments according to precise volume standards. The buildings bend slightly at each end to give the original rectangular shape a more dynamic form. Ribbon windows make a strong impact along the facades, divided by brick partitions. Circular structures form a further storey on the roof. On the north east side of the area, Adalberto Libera experimented with a design based on a two-storey cross layout (drawing). The central block contains a staircase positioned diagonally with adjacent pedestrian walkways leading to 4 apartments whose internal layouts are aligned with the external perimeter walls. The elegance of composition and design rules combine and blend naturally with the surrounding landscape, to become an integral part of the project.

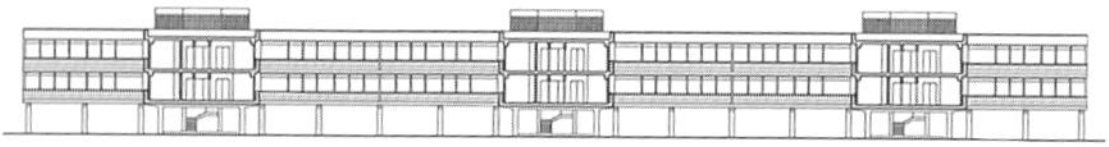

architects
Straight line buildings:
Vittorio Cafiero,
Adalberto Libera, Amedeo
Lucchichenti, Vincenzo
Monaco, Luigi Moretti
Cross-shaped buildings:
Adalberto Libera

type
residential

construction
Straight line buildings:
1957-1960
Cross-shaped buildings:
1958-1960

37. Parco della Musica: Auditorium and Museo Aristaios

Parco della Musica Auditorium:
viale Pietro De Coubertin 30
00196 Rome

Winter
Mon - Sat / 11 am - 6 pm
Sun / 10 am - 6 pm
Summer
Mon - Sat / 11 am - 8 pm
Sun / 10 am - 8 pm

+39 06 80241281
visiteguidate@
musicaperroma.it
www.auditorium.com

53 / 168 / 910 / 982 / n3d > De Coubertin / Auditorium

The Parco della Musica Auditorium was built in the heart of the Olympic Village by Renzo Piano Building Workshop. It is composed of three independent structures or "sound boxes" – sala Petrassi, sala Sinopoli and sala Santa Cecilia. They are symmetrically arranged to provide maximum flexibility and are surrounded by an open space that conceals the Cavea, an amphitheatre for concerts and events seating 3,000 spectators. The project includes a musical instrument museum, office space, and a specialised library. Work began in 1995 after the discovery of the foundations of a Roman Villa dating to the 6th century B.C. which is an integrated part of the complex and is visible from the underground foyer entrance to the concert halls. A blend of materials was used to create the vision of an "architectural orchestra". Travertine stone, used for the Cavea and the main entrances combines with the vertical brick surfaces, and the pre-oxidised lead roofing on the concert halls. Following acoustic research, it was decided to use wood as the main material including internal structures that can be dismantled, recalling the construction of an arc or a lute. The Auditorium was inaugurated in 2002 on the date of the birth of Rome.

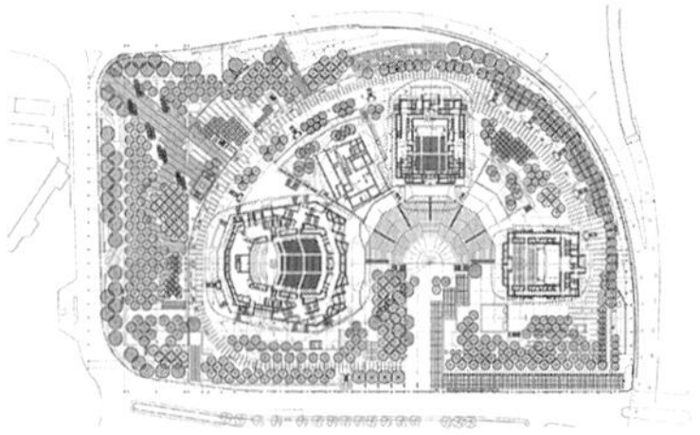

© Renzo Piano Building Workshop

Zweiger / Shutterstock.com

architects
Renzo Piano Building Workshop

type
auditorium

construction
1995-2002

Museo Aristaios:
viale Pietro De Coubertin 30
00196 Rome

Winter
Mon - Sat / 11 am - 6 pm
Sun / 10 am - 6 pm
Summer
Mon - Sat / 11 am - 8 pm
Sun / 10 am - 8 pm

+39 06 80241281
visiteguidate@
musicaperroma.it
www.auditorium.com

In 2012, Alvisi Kirimoto staged the 161 pieces collection donated by Maestro Giuseppe Sinopoli, on display in the Sala del "Peduncolo" at the Auditorium di Roma.
The excellent display allows visitors to discover the archaeological finds dating between 3200 B.C. and 300 B.C.
Two suspended showcases measuring 24 × 7 metres long, contain most of the pieces, arranged at different heights and depths for greater visual effect. Eleven cylindrical showcases positioned along the axis of the ancient Roman walls visible outdoors below, represent a "small archaeological forest" – tempting visitors towards further exploration.

53 / 168 / 910 / 982 / n3d > De Coubertin / Auditorium

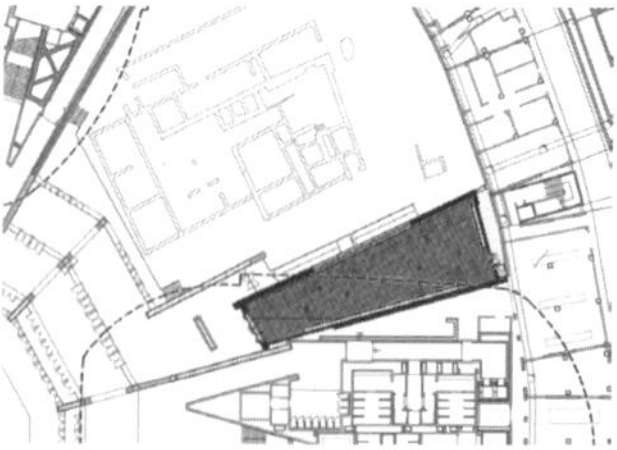

architects
Alvisi Kirimoto

type
museo

construction
2012

38. Olympic Sports Arena

piazza Apollodoro 10
00196 Rome

open to the public

+39 06 540901
info@alleventsspa.it
www.palazzodellosportroma.it

2 > Flaminia / Reni

168 / 910 / n3s > De Coubertin / Palazzetto dello Sport

Nervi went through a second period of creative research focussed on the use of ferro-cement and natural prefabrication methods. The 'Palazzetto dello Sport' is one of his finest examples. Designed to be replicated in other cities, and as a symbol of the 1960 Olympics, it exemplified figurative and dynamic plastic strength, and reinvented structural design for large sports arenas. The building rises from the ground in the form of a slightly flattened, completely ribbed structure. The dome is sustained by 36 Y-shaped external supports with strong visual impact, and inside, is designed to attract the attention of the spectators where the natural light is the dominant feature. The roof is composed of 1620 prefabricated diamond-shaped elements in ferro-cement, dismantled into segments for on-site assembly on lightweight sections of scaffolding, by placing the reinforcing in the exact positions before the final casting. The Olympic Sports Arena confirms Nervi's reputation as one of the best engineers on the modern international scene, and demonstrates his desire to experiment with new forms using innovative construction techniques.

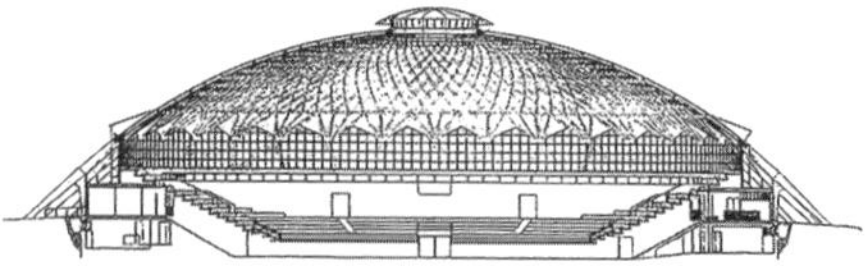

architects
Pier Luigi Nervi,
Annibale Vitellozzi

type
sport complex

construction
1956-1957

39. MAXXI

via Guido Reni 4A
00196 Rome

Tue - Sun / 11 am - 7 pm
First Sunday of each month / 11 am - 10 pm
Mon / closed

+39 06 3201954
infopoint@fondazionemaxxi.it
www.maxxi.art

168 > Maxxi

"Architecture should provide pleasure and the public should perceive a feeling of harmony".
This is the principle expressed by Zaha Hadid, which she applied to the construction of the MAXXI National museum of 21st-century arts. This innovative architectural solution is her interpretation of the museum of the 21st century, located in a quarter previously occupied by factories and parts of the ex Montello military barracks. The dynamic building is well integrated in a limited context and the contrast between interior and exterior underlines the relationship with the urban fabric. The external spaces were designed considering the restoration of part of the barracks, and raised elements incorporate sections of the previous military pavilions. The ground floor welcomes visitors with an entrance foyer, a bookshop, a gallery, and an auditorium. Suspended steel stairs rise from this floor to the upper storeys. Glazed corridors connect the exhibition galleries and roofing with steel partitions and sun breakers, providing ample luminosity in a blend of natural and artificial lighting. Fluid lines and curved angles are emphasised with the use of exposed raw concrete in perfect harmony with the surrounding modern constructions.

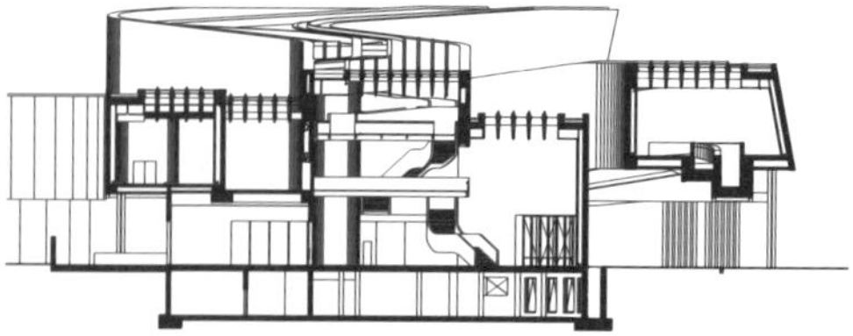

© Zaha Hadid Architects

architects	**type**	**construction**
Zaha Hadid Architects	museum	2003-2010

40. Apartment Building in via San Valentino

via di San Valentino 16
00197 Rome

external viewing only

52 > Archimede

This building in via San Valentino was the first collaboration between Amedeo Lucchenti and Vincenzo Monaco, and with the view of Spider Man, Hulk, Batman and a white figure climbing up the facades, we are plunged into a world of superheroes. In reality, this was one of the best examples of apartment buildings created in the 1950s. The result of twenty years of architectural research, this apartment building, constructed in 1953, with a plaster render finish, has access stairs and elevator positioned in the centre of the structure leading up six floors with two apartments per floor. The internal layouts include dining and living rooms overlooking the street. The facades are finished in rough render similar to raw concrete, with wooden detailing, while the loggias and full height windows provide extra lighting, as well as creating a harmonious effect in direct contact between interior and exterior. To the rear, a second block is more enclosed and houses the bedrooms and bathrooms. The rooftop completes this integration with nature, and the attic floor is designed with a curved profile in contrast with the regular geometry of the layout and facades.

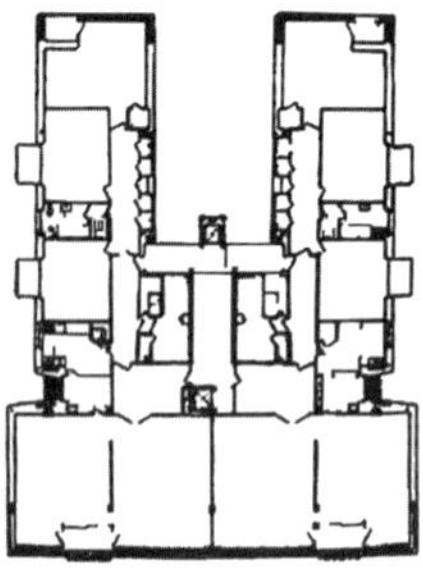

architects
Amedeo Luccichenti,
Vincenzo Monaco

type
residential

construction
1952-1953

41. Basilica del Sacro Cuore Immacolato di Maria

piazza Euclide
00197 Rome

open to the public

+39 06 8070359

www.parrocchiacuoreimma-colatodimaria.it

230 > Sacro Cuore di Maria / Euclide

Known as "the Basilica without a dome", this church dominates the area where five streets merge in piazza Euclide in the Parioli quarter. It was an ongoing construction site for about thirty years. The project was modified by Armando Brasini several times until he decided on a layout incorporating a Latin cross and Greek cross within a circle. An elaborate facade features columns in front of and surrounding the basilica. As well as its formal aspect, the building has a majestic design. The original project for the foundations provided for four huge central pillars to sustain a large dome, for which excavations were dug deep enough to contain the current crypt measuring 42 by 16 metres with a height of 6.6 metres, above the foundation level. The floor slabs covering the crypt are also supported by 34 reinforced concrete pillars. Inside the pronaos with its travertine stone columns and carved pediment, the centre space is surrounded by four octagonal side chapels and a narthex with paintings showing the baptism of Christ. The apse, 26 metres in diameter, was designed to be in proportion with the future dome, which was not constructed but replaced with a drum that made the basilica the highest visible reference point from the surrounding hills.

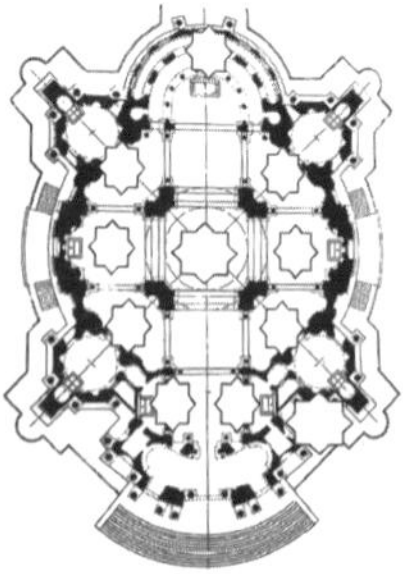

© Luca Farinelli

architects
Armando Brasini

type
church

construction
1923-1951

42. Mosque and Islamic Cultural Centre

viale della Moschea 85
00199 Rome

Wed - Sat / 9 am - 12 am

+39 06 8082258
segreteria.66centroislamico@
hotmail.it

230 > Moschea / Forte Antenne

Inaugurated in 1995, the Islamic Cultural Centre of Rome and largest mosque in Europe is the most important reference point for the Muslim community in Italy. The centre is extremely versatile, incorporating a library, congress centre and a language school. Traditional Islamic design adapts well to western formal architecture and modular regularity. Local models and materials are used to express a certain type of culture, but even more so, an ideology. The wall surfaces are faced with smoothed bricks combined with strips of travertine and grey peperino stone. Designed by Paolo Portoghesi, Vittorio Gigliotti and Sami Mousawi, the Mosque and the Cultural Centre are composed of different sections connected by long narrow porticos that lead to two open circular spaces at each end. The main layout is centred around the rectangular space that forms the prayer hall. Each section is composed of a square unit covered by smaller vaultings that converge towards the central dome. The structural support columns and ribbing are in reinforced concrete, subjected to combined compressive and bending action, generating a continuous pattern of woven lines through which the light is filtered to create new perspective effects.

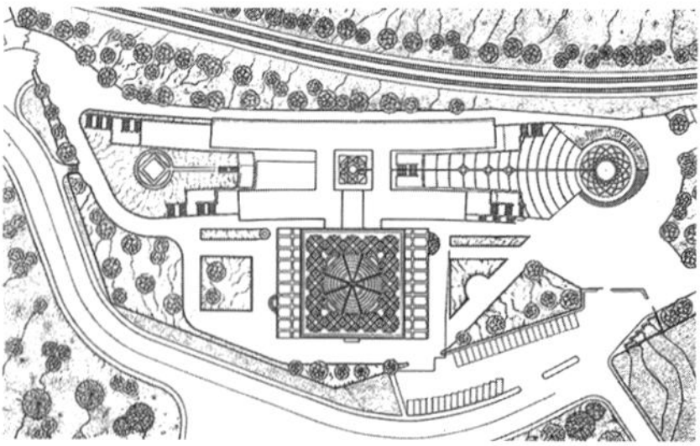

architects
Paolo Porthoghesi, Vittorio Gigliotti, Sami Mousawi

type
mosque, cultural centre

construction
1995

43. La Nave Apartment Building

via Fratelli Ruspoli 10-12
00198 Rome

external viewing only

168 > Lima

Rational architectural design in the 1950s was the starting point for a new field of experimentation for the construction of the La Nave apartment building. Located in via Fratelli Ruspoli, it is well-known for its angular perspective, and is composed of two independent structures, one enclosed within the other forming the courtyard. The external structure emphasises the decision to focus on articulated use of the exterior surfaces. The ribbon windows are visibly interrupted in the corners where the projecting balconies recall the prow of a ship, in contrast with the common strictly formal design of apartment buildings, and with the construction style in the surrounding neighbourhood. Although positioned coherently in an urban plot respecting its shape, the building's relationship with its context is particularly striking on the rear facade where the regular geometry of the internal layout gives a glimpse of intimate functional interiors. The six story facades are finished in travertine stone and light grey plaster render, with metal details in balcony railings, indicative of research into different construction materials.

architects
Ugo Luccichenti

type
residential

construction
1949

44. Il Girasole Apartment Building

viale Bruno Buozzi 64
00197 Rome

external viewing only

52 > Buozzi / Micheli

Located in the Parioli quarter, Il Girasole apartment building, also called Girasole House, was designed by the rationalist architect, Luigi Moretti. The distinctive element is the long slit down the main facade that divides the building into two sections, underlining the asymmetry of the crowning element: an irregular gable that embodies a reinterpretation of the classical archetype in Rationalist style. The base, clad in Tivoli travertine stone, represents little more than a podium on which the two sections are set, divided by the vertical slit. In certain points, the finish on the travertine stone surface seems almost rough, to give a less contrived effect. The vertical slit sheds light into the stairways and accesses to the different apartments, while the side facades feature oblique zigzag panels that increase the internal lighting. This reinterpretation of classical architecture became the distinctive signature of one of Moretti's most famous works in the capital.

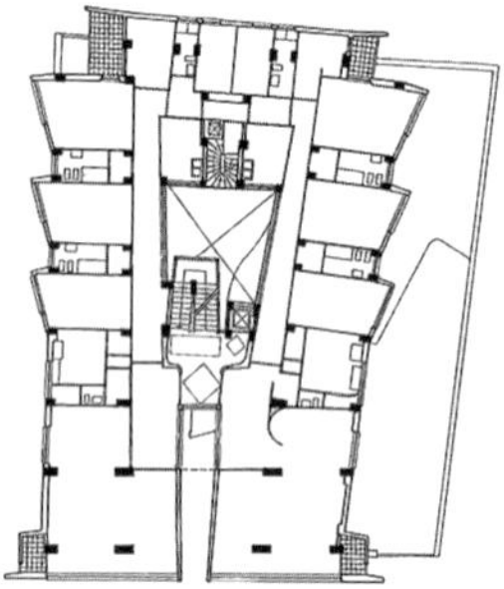

architects
Luigi Moretti

type
residential

construction
1950

45. Egyptian Academy Redevelopment and Restoration

via Omero 4
00197 Rome

open to the public

+39 06 3201896
+39 06 3201907
info@accademiaegitto.it
www.accademiaegitto.org

3 > Valle Giulia
2 / 3 / 19 > Galleria Arte Moderna

Immersed in Villa Borghese park in the green Valle Giulia, the Egyptian Academy was first constructed in 1966, and in 2012, underwent extensive restoration work that changed the whole aspect of the building. The structure has become the symbol of the cultural bond among peoples, and through the restoration and expansion of the museum, the new image is aimed at a reinterpretation of Egyptian symbology in a contemporary version. The facade is clad in stone tiles carved with Egyptian hieroglyphics. An interesting aspect was the choice to leave certain original elements, such as the original crowning cornice on one of the buildings which is perfectly coherent with the design of the contemporary project. The building houses the first Egyptian Museum in Rome with a collection of priceless pieces from the principle museums in Egypt.

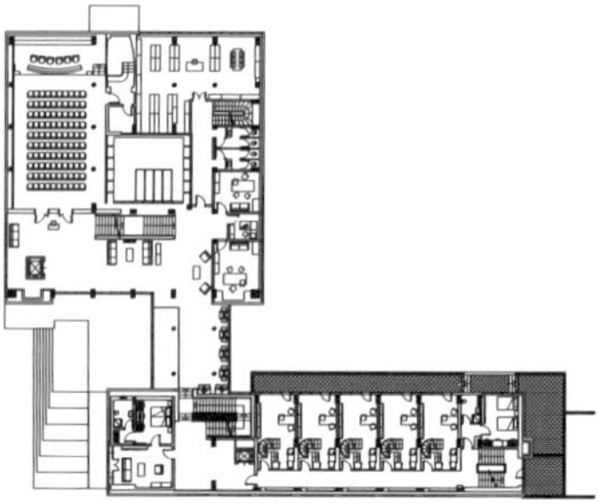

© Studio Linea, Alfredo Benedetti

architects
Benedetto Todaro, Roberto Palumbo, Quasar Progetto. Coordinamento generale: Carlo Maggini (Studio Linea), Alfredo Benedetti, Luca Leonori, Emanuele Mantrici (Studiokami)

type
library, museum, academy, auditorium

construction
2012

46. Villa Borghese. Gallery and Underground Parking

Borghese Gallery: piazzale Scipione Borghese 5
Underground Parking: viale del Galoppatoio 33
00197 Rome

Tue - Sun / 9 am - 7 pm
Mon / closed

+39 0632810
galleria borghese
+39 068413979
ga-bor@beniculturali.it
www.galleriaborghese.beniculturali.it

52 / 53 / 63 / 83 / 92 / 223 / 360 / 910 / n92 > Pinciana / Museo Borghese

Recognised as one of the most important museums in Rome, the Borghese Gallery was built in the 17th century as a private residence, but was converted to a state museum in the early 20th century. One of the most fascinating architectural elements is the double entrance staircase, a reconstruction of the original stairs that were dismantled in the late 18th century because of ground sinking. While the main facade at ground level is focussed on the central portico, the upper floor has a terrace with a richly carved and decorated background. The interior is an explosion of multi-coloured marble and stucco decoration that creates a perfect setting for the museum collection. To create easier traffic flow to the museum, an underground parking area was built by Luigi Moretti and Renzo Rosi (Società Condotte) in the 1960s, in the form of a huge space with supporting columns. The columns provide strong visual impact, as do the ventilation systems and access routes. This is an infrastructure, not designed simply for practicality, but as a space to stroll around and enjoy, discovering patios and spiral staircases concealed by lawns that create continuity with the Villa Borghese gardens.

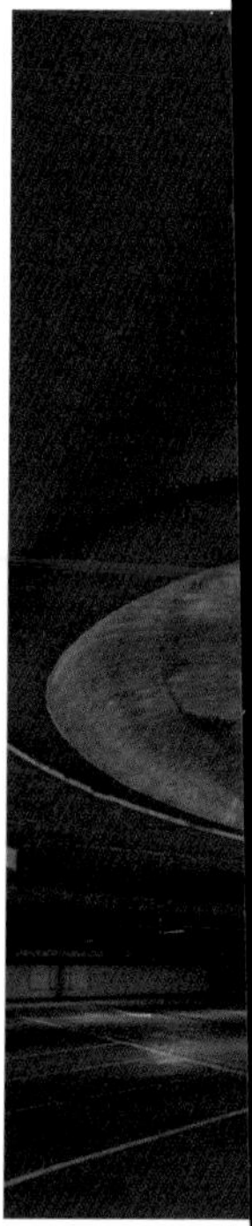

© Luca Farinelli

architects
Borghese Gallery:
Flaminio Ponzio
Underground Parking:
Luigi Moretti, Renzo Rosi
(Società Condotte)

type
museum, parking

construction
Borghese Gallery:
1607-1620
Underground Parking:
1966-1972

47. La Rinascente in piazza Fiume

piazza Fiume
00198 Rome

Mon - Sat / 9 am - 9 pm
Sun / 10 am - 9 pm

+39 06 8841231

www.rinascente.it

223 / 360 / 63 / 83 / 92 / n92 > Fiume

The large Rinascente department store is perfectly integrated in the surrounding urban and historic fabric of the city, combining the simplicity of modern architecture with classic construction methods. The granular surface and colour of the facades recall the Baroque period, creating a play of light and shade. The cornices and the attached discontinuous metal beam sections are recognised features present in classical Roman architecture. Inspired by ancient moulding, the projecting string courses are quite visible and also provide a practical function for draining rain water. The contrasting construction styles can be seen in the prefabricated steel panels that act as cornices for the granite and red marble cladding, recessed behind the metal grids. Inside the building, the floors are open space and all nine storeys, including the three basement floors, are connected by a sinuous, light steel, helical staircase whose main structural load is borne by the perimeter walls. The comprehensive geometrical effect accentuates the Rational style of this rectangular block located in Piazza Fiume, urban nerve centre between via Salaria and corso d'Italia, near the Aurelian Walls.

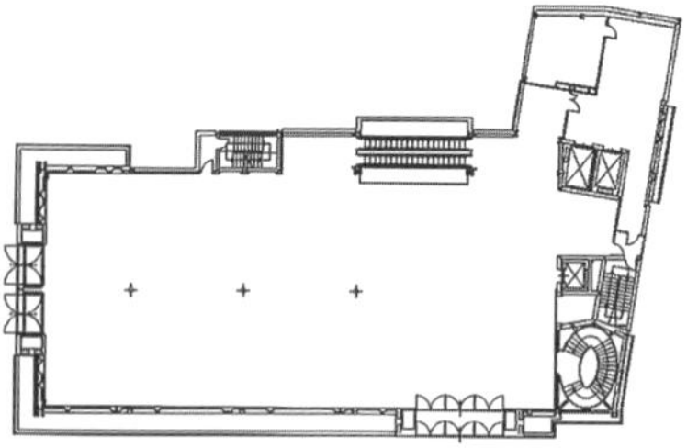

© Luca Farinelli

architects
Franco Albini, Franca Helg

type
retail

construction
1957-1961

48. MACRO

via Nizza 138
00198 Rome

Tue - Fri / 10 am - 8 pm
Sun / 10 am - 8 pm
Sat / 10 am - 10 pm
Mon / closes

+39 06 696271
info.macro@palaexpo.it
www.museomacro.it

38 / 89 > Nizza/V.le Margherita

The new museum of contemporary art is located on the corner of via Nizza and via Cagliari, where surrounding 19th century buildings are reflected in its glazed facades. This dynamic, controversial building in reinforced concrete, steel, and metal fibre laminated glass, draws the public into an interior dominated by red, black and white. The urban space is directly connected to the building through the double height foyer crossed by ramps and suspended corridors; an enclosed red volume acts as a small educational auditorium, while the empty spaces above are used as exhibition walls for hanging art works. The promenade continues through three internal piazzas, while another entrance on the top level, with terrace and restaurant, is accessible from the street providing visitors with a view of the contemporary landscape. Sections of linear surfaces blend with a mechanism to create a dynamic architectural sequence: torsion and translation of rectangular spaces make this area unique. The strong impact of these shapes underline the dynamic internal and external sections, generating spaces that are cohesive, but which provoke a feeling of disorientation in a space that is so regular while incorporating irregular composition and design.

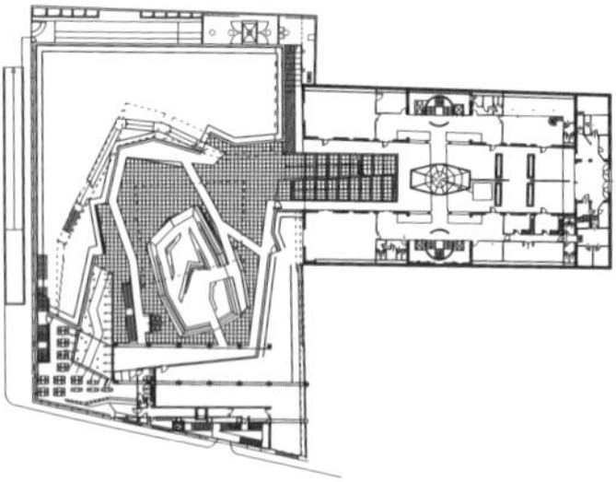

architects
Studio Odile Decq

type
museum

construction
2002

49. Annibaliano B1 Metro Station

piazza Annibaliano
00100 Rome

Mon - Sun /
5.30 am - 11.30 pm

B1 > S. Agnese / Annibaliano

38 / 80 / 88 >
S. Agnese / Annibaliano

The Annibaliano Station on the B1 Subway line in the north east area of the city is one of the stations on the B1 line extension in its urban section. The main objective is to reduce road traffic on the Grande Raccordo Anulare (Ring Road) and to increase public accessibility in the so-called "oltre Aniene" area. The station is immediately recognisable for the exposed concrete structures that emerge from the underground piazza. The monumental nature of the station signals the presence of the infrastructure hub with its strong impact, as it does at the Libia and Conca D'Oro Stations. Three arterial roads – via Asmara, via Bressanone, corso Trieste – are the primary accesses to an open-air area that forms the new important hub for the surrounding urban zones. Completely constructed in prefabricated reinforced concrete, the curved form echoes the monumental surroundings. The subway station is equipped with elevators and escalators that connect the pavement to an intermediate public services level, then continuing down to the subway track level. The station represents a new open space incorporating a public park area in the piazza Annibaliano neighbourhood.

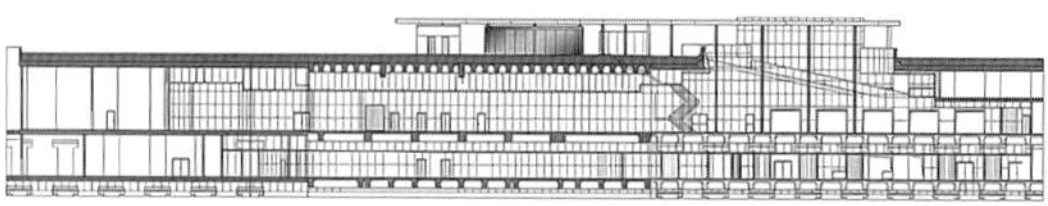

architects
ABDR Architetti Associati

type
subway station

construction
2013

50. Jonio B1 Metro Station

via Scarpanto 22-26
00139 Rome

Mon - Sun /
5.30 am - 11.30 pm

With its rhythmic use of elementary forms, this project by Studio Purini-Thermes for the Jonio B1 subway station was designed to be integrated into the city system as part of the urban fabric. The project space is enclosed in red panelling that encircles the curved lines of the structure, interrupted by steel and glass sections that provide access to the station from via Scarpanto. Inside the structure is a parking area, into which air and light are filtered through grids in the facade. Elements linked with the city and a roof garden provide the local neighbourhood with an open public green park space. Geometrical structures in the garden create light wells into the internal parking area. In fact, light is one of the main features inside the station where extensive white areas have been used as an instrument to increase luminosity.

63 / 69 / 338 / 351 / 435 / C5 / NMB1
> Jonio

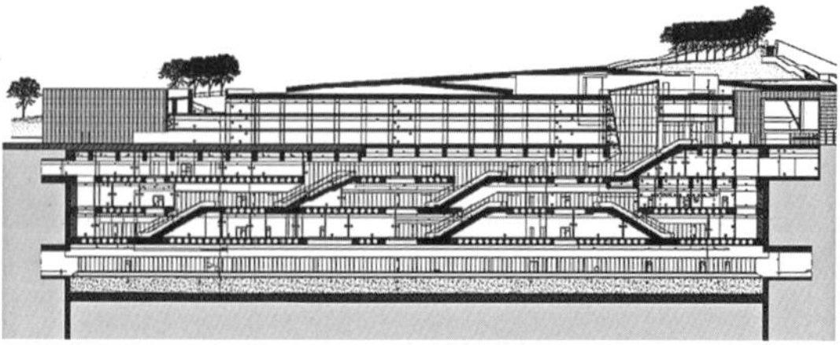

architects
Studio Purini-Thermes

type
subway station

construction
2009-2014

51. Restoration of Villa Blanc

via Nomentana 216
00162 Rome

open to the public

+39 06 852251

www.luiss.it

B1 > S.Agnese/
Annibaliano

60 / 66 / 82 / 90 >
Nomentana/S.Agnese

A fine example of late 19th century eclectic architecture, Villa Blanc is the result of extensive restoration of the "house of delight" built by Marquis Lorenzo Lezzani, who sold the property and its garden to Baron Alberto de Blanc, who commissioned the architect Giacomo Boni; it was the close association between these two men that led to the completion of this unique restoration. Left in a state of complete abandon, the property was purchased in 1997 by the LUISS University for the headquarters of the LUISS Business School. The restoration project was assigned to Massimo Picciotto who managed to reveal all the original features of the property through careful recovery of the artistic elements of the building. Thanks to this recent intervention, it was possible to focus on highlighting the original features, including the beautiful gardens which are enjoyed not only by the LUISS School, but by the entire neighbourhood.

architects
Massimo Picciotto

type
university

construction
2012-2017

52. Papanice House

via Giuseppe Marchi 3
00161 Rome

external viewing only

168 / 310 / 445 / 542 / nMB1 > XXVI aprile / Nardini

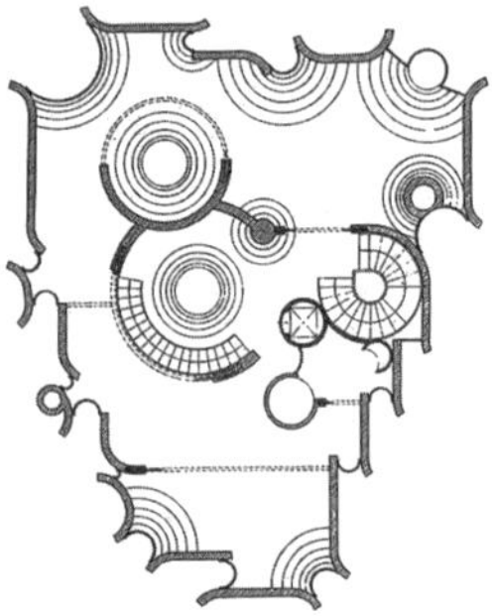

This important project designed by Paolo Portoghesi and engineer, Vittorio Gigliotti, represents the new approach to design in the sixties and seventies that combined the passion for the Roman Baroque style with research into new spatial plasticism. Divided into four storeys, one of which is a basement floor, the house includes a small attic space on the roof. Many facades of the house are clad in semi-circular vertical majolica panels, recalling elements of nature. Concave and converse external walls determine the curved layout of the entire internal space. Internal walls are painted with horizontal stripes, and series of concentric forms add great impact to the ceilings in the living room. By curving one wall, and placing two identical curved walls adjacent to it, the architect was able to create an intrinsic spatial extension visible from various viewpoints. The curved line became the fil rouge of the project, able to unite architecture, nature, function and organic form.

architects
Paolo Portoghesi,
Vittorio Gigliotti

type
residential

construction
1966-1970

53. Zaccardi Apartment Building

via Giovanni Battista De Rossi 12
00161 Rome

external viewing only

B / B1 > Bologna

60 / 66 / 82 / n66 / n90 > Nomentana/Villa Torlonia

The Zaccardi building in via Giovan Battista De Rossi is located in the Nomentano quarter. Composed of two distinct independent sections, from the exterior, it gives an impression of a strong formal separation. The larger building is set at right angles in the plot while the other has a curved form that permits the inclusion of rhomboid shaped balconies, one of the main design features, that also provide direct sunlight. The colours chosen for the facades identify the various sections: white for the regular sections, containing two apartments per floor, pink for the building with the projecting balconies, which have a single apartment on each floor. Structurally the two buildings are connected by a long reinforced concrete beam and are united by a single, deep, and completely glazed entrance foyer. This modern design combines Rationalist architecture with simple organic elements. The constructive and architectural details add to the formal and spatial composition of this building: ceramic planters, metal railings, and glass balustrades, that create effects of light and shade, perfectly coherent with the modest internal spaces.

© Luca Farinelli

architects
Mario Ridolfi,
Wolfgang Frankl

type
residential

construction
1951

0 m
200 m
500 m
S. Agnese/ Annibaliano
Mausoleo di Tor di Quinto
Parrocchia di Sant'Angela Merici
Basilica di Sant'Agnese fuori le Mura
Mausoleo di Santa Costanza
Via Annone
Corso Trieste
Via di S. Costanza
Piazza Giovanni Winckelmann
Via Rodolfo Lanciani
Via dei Monti di Pietralata
Via Giulio Curio
Via dei Monti Tiburtini
Circonvallazione Nomentana
Viale Gorizia
Via Tolmino
Via Nomentana
Via Carlo Fea
Via Oreste Tommasini
Via degli Appenini
Parrocchia di Santa Francesca Cabrini
ORMA Atelier
Largo di Villa Massimo
Viale XXI Aprile
Via di Villa Ricotti
Falsi Ruderi
Tempio di Saturno
Casino Dei Principi
Musei di Villa Torlonia
La Casina delle Civette
Villa Torlonia
Campo da Tornei
Serra Moresca
Bologna
Via Ravenna
Via Livorno
Via Stamira
Via Lorenzo il Magnifico
Nuova Circonvallazione Interna
Villino Ximenes
Villino Rosso
Piazza Galeno
Piazza Ruggero di Sicilia
Via di S. Ippolito
Piazza Salerno
Teatro Italia
Museo Parigino
Via Catania
Roma Tiburtina
Piazzale delle Provincie
Piazzale degli Eroi
Policlinico
Via Treviso
Viale Ippocrate
Via Cupa
Via Tiburtina
Prato della Facoltà di Ingegneria
Policlinico Umberto I
Museo di Zoologia
Viale Regina Elena
Via del Castro Laurenziano
Tangenziale Est
Museo di Storia della Medicina
Museo dell'Arte Contemporanea MLAC - Sapienza
Museo di Chimica Primo Levi
Basilica di San Lorenzo fuori le mura
Museo della Matematica
Museo di Antropologia G. Sergi - Sapienza
Cimitero Monumentale del Verano
Via dei Frentani
Via dei Ramni
Circonvallazione Tiburtina

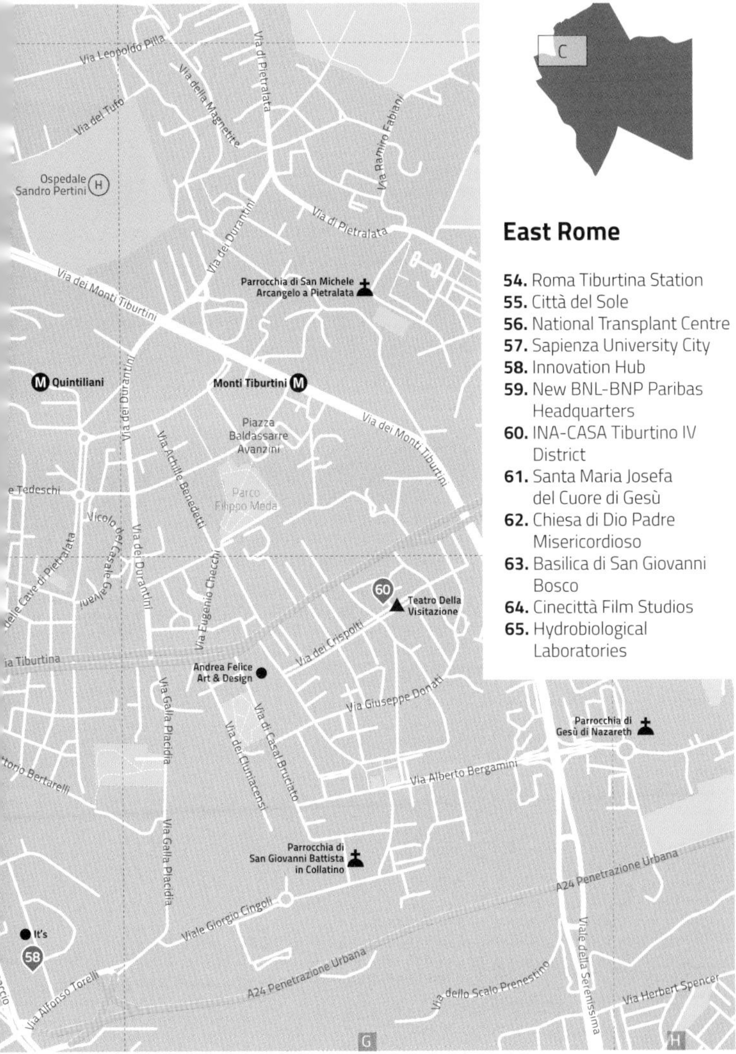

East Rome

54. Roma Tiburtina Station
55. Città del Sole
56. National Transplant Centre
57. Sapienza University City
58. Innovation Hub
59. New BNL-BNP Paribas Headquarters
60. INA-CASA Tiburtino IV District
61. Santa Maria Josefa del Cuore di Gesù
62. Chiesa di Dio Padre Misericordioso
63. Basilica di San Giovanni Bosco
64. Cinecittà Film Studios
65. Hydrobiological Laboratories

54. Roma Tiburtina Station

piazzale della Stazione Tiburtina
00162 Rome

open to the public

www.stazioneromatiburtina.it

409 > Stazione Tiburtina

The new Tiburtina Station multimodal transport hub was designed to develop existing rail systems to High Speed rail services, and form a new urban transit centre.
Respecting the existing rail system, the bridge structure of Tiburtina Station connects the districts of Nomentano and Pietralata, previously divided by the railway lines. This infrastructure has boosted the national and regional railway systems, and has provided a public piazza and new multimodal transit connections. The 25 station platforms are covered by a pedestrian gallery, proposed as an urban boulevard with a 19th century flavour, but built using technological innovations. A lattice girder, 350 metres long and 60 metres wide, supported by pillars, covers the public platform and conceals all the technical services. Eight sinuous, semitransparent structures in Corian and Alicrite are suspended from the girder to house a VIP lounge, a WI-FI area, offices and restaurants. For statics reasons, these rooms project from the long glass facade, making them visible on arrival at the station. The structural, energy and bio-climatic choices earned the project the Eurosolar Italia prize in 2002.

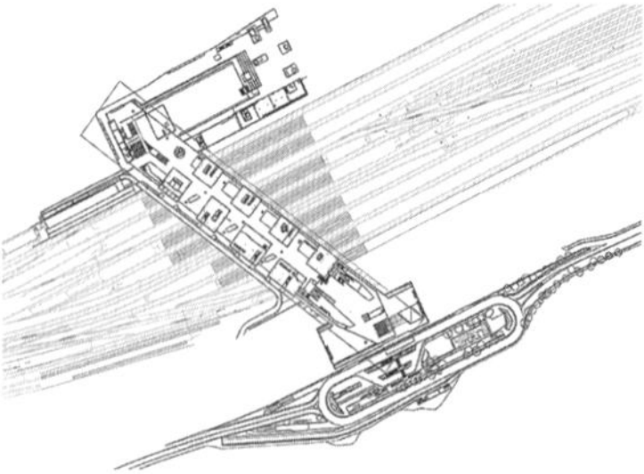

© ABDR Architetti Associati

architects
ABDR Architetti Associati

type
railway station

construction
2011

55. Città del Sole

via della Lega Lombarda,
via Arduino
00162 Rome

partially open to the public

490 / 495 / 649 / nMB
> Lega Lombarda

Winner of a competition by invitation, the Città del Sole project is part of a Programme Agreement set up to redevelop the former deposit land belonging to ATAC, the city council public transport service. Città del Sole occupies the area, integrating well with the surrounding urban fabric, as can be seen at the entrance piazza of the complex that is linked with the access to the Tiburtino II district. The structure is not separated from the neighbourhood, and the base podiums of the residential constructions represent direct contact with the ground and with public and private buildings. The first block is two storeys high with retail stores and a library, while a management centre is housed on the first floor. The complex is composed of three structures, one for office space, the second contains eight duplex town houses, while the third, a 9-storey tower block, houses 72 apartments, with loggias. The facade elements are practical and functional: on the ground floor, there are long glass windows for maximum light, while the first floor facades feature sun screens to protect the office interiors, and louvre aluminium shutters on the residential blocks permit occupants to control sunlight.

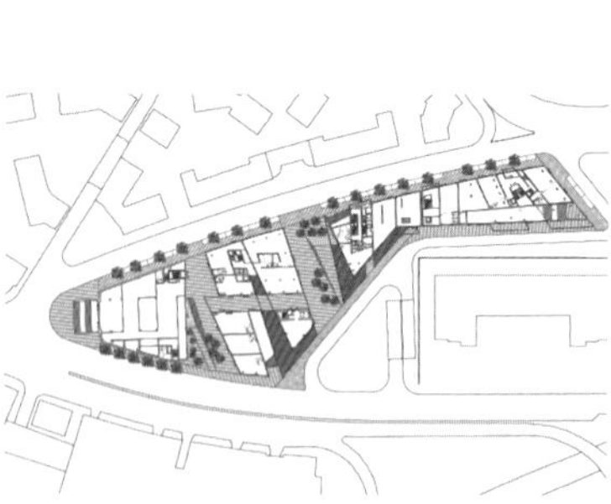

© Labics

architects
Labics

type
offices, retail, residential

construction
2010-2016

56. National Transplant Centre

via Giano della Bella 34
00162 Rome

partially open to the public

120F / 490 / 495 / 542 / 649 / P10 / P20 / nMB > Provincie

"Natural light interacts extensively with architecture and can become a simple architectural element." This is the architectural principle that defines the National Transplant Centre opened in 2016. The project design is composed of a habitat for light, whose force is projected towards the exterior through a glass structure that forms an entrance foyer. Every tiny detail has been researched to guarantee work place efficiency in this small rectangular space. The light airy effect of the steel and glass section contrasts with the solid aspect of the green tiled walls of the main building. Square windows arranged in an irregular pattern, are recessed into the walls and framed in marble. This allows the light to fill the interior, composed of white plaster walls and white furnishings in perfect harmony with the wooden parquet flooring on one side and the polished grey surface on the other. The office spaces are raised above the ground floor that houses a large co-working table and long lines of bookcases that partition the two areas.

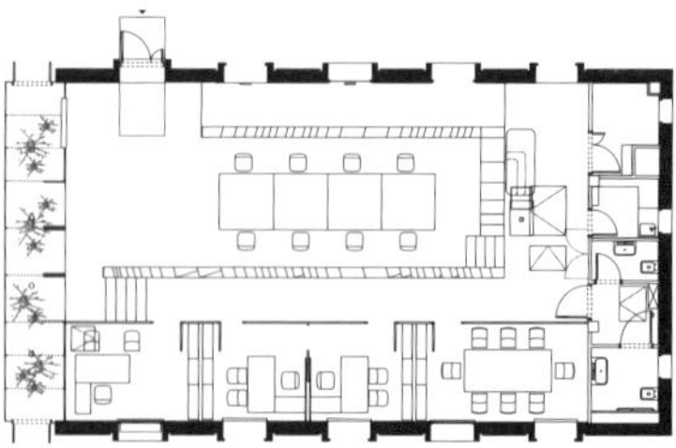

© IaN+

architects
IaN+ (Arch. Carmelo Baglivo,
Arch. Luca Galofaro,
Ing. Stefania Manna,
Coll. Arch. Gianluca Fontana)

type
research centre

construction
2015

57. Sapienza University City

piazzale Aldo Moro 1-5
00185 Rome

partially open to the public

2 / 3 / 19 > Università La Sapienza o Regina Elena / V.le Università

B / B1 > Policlinico

88 / n3s > Università La Sapienza o Regina Elena / V.le Università

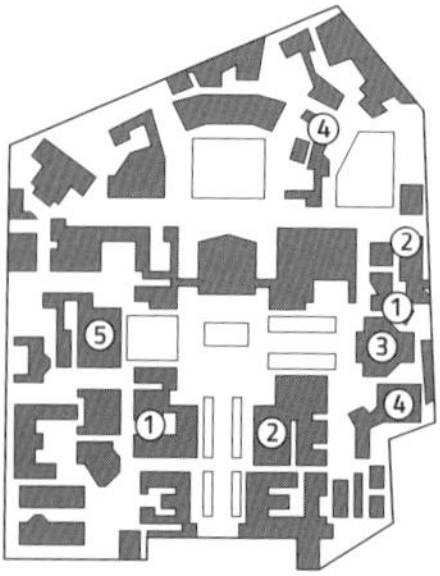

The main centre of the Sapienza University occupies a large area between the Policlinico and the Verano cemetery, along via Nomentana. The layout represents a combination of different solutions based on Marcello Piacentini's idea of applying US university campus architectural trends in an Italian rationalist context, with its inherent traditions. The concept of the ancient Roman forum is combined with the social need for conviviality in spaces that are not necessarily regular, but are harmonious, well-balanced, and rich in green areas. The complex is based on the Latin Cross basilica layout with a monumental entrance and a central axis that separates the buildings that were built over a 5-year period: the Physics Department (Giuseppe Pagano), Chemistry Department (Pietro Aschieri), Mathematics Department (Gio Ponti), Pharmaceutical Chemistry and Botany Department (Giuseppe Capponi) all on the right hand side, and the Mineralogy, Geology and Palaeontology Department (Giovanni Michelucci) on the left. The transept is composed of piazzale della Minerva overlooked by the Rector's building, with the main auditorium and library, which are raised above the entrance level.
1 / Physics Department; 2 / Chemistry Department; 3 / Mathematics Department; 4 / Pharmaceutical Chemistry and Botany Department; 5 / Mineralogy, Geology and Palaeontology Institute.

architects
Urban development: Marcello Piacentini / Physics Department: Giuseppe Pagano / Chemistry Department: Pietro Aschieri / Mathematics Department: Gio Ponti / Pharmaceutical Chemistry and Botany Department: Giuseppe Capponi / Mineralogy, Geology and Palaeontology Institute: Giovanni Michelucci / Chapel of Divine Wisdom: Marcello Piacentini

type
university

construction
Urban development: 1932-1935 / Physics Department: 1933-1935 / Chemistry Department: 1932-1938 / Mathematics Department: 1934-1935 / Pharmaceutical Chemistry and Botany Department: 1933-1935 / Mineralogy, Geology and Palaeontology Institute: 1933-1935 / Chapel of Divine Wisdom: 1950-1951

58. Innovation Hub

via Pettinengo 72
00159 Rome

partially open to the public

409 / n409 >
Portonaccio / Galliano

An Innovation Hub is the main office of the young architectural firm, It's, who designed the building, is located near the Tiburtina railway station. The project was designed to "trigger an evolutionary development for renewal in the area." The Hub introduces a different scale of architectural research in a district where new urban experimentation is currently underway. The idea was to combine the architects' work with that of other innovative start-up activities, through the use of BIM software and prefabricated elements in a single building. The piazza in front of the building is the core of the urban redevelopment process, organised to display innovative projects. The three-storey building is on a raised site, 10 metres above street level. It has a wooden frame structure, clad with corrugated aluminium panels to recall the industrial nature of the area. Inside, prefabricated cross-laminated xlam panel partitions guarantee adequate energy efficiency for workspace activities, and solar panels on the roof reduce energy consumption. The project won the BIM&DIGITAL Award 2017, for the techniques employed and reduced construction time.

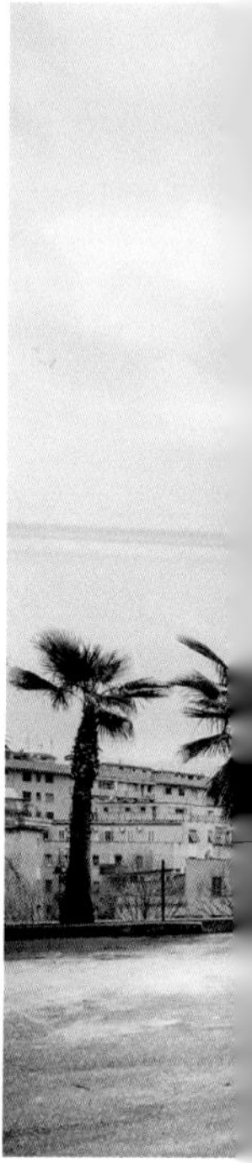

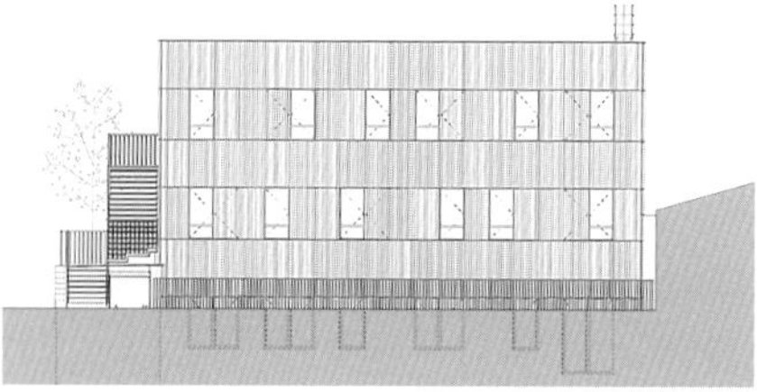

architects
It's

type
research centre

construction
2017-2019

59. New BNL-BNP Paribas Headquarters

via Tiburtina 399
00157 Rome

external viewing only

AV / REG > Stazione Roma Tiburtina

111 / 111F / 120F / 163 / 211 / 309 / 441 / 448 / n041 / nMB > Tiburtina / Portonaccio

The Orizzonte Europa Building, new BNL-BNP Paribas headquarters, is a completely glazed structure that has become a landmark in the Tiburtino district. The concept was designed to "reflect the sky while distorting it": and on first sight, the linear layout and fragmented surfaces of the facade creates enormous impact. The interior covers 75,000 square metres and applies the latest principles of smart working and technological open space, achieved through horizontal activity distribution. As well as the office space that makes up the central core, the building also contains a training centre, auditorium, restaurant, car park, infirmary, nursery school, and gym, a welfare system that connects the division between private life and the community. The curved entrance was designed to create a frame for the historic water tower designed by renowned architect, Mazzoni. The building presents a scenic backdrop that changes constantly with the weather and the light, thanks to the facade composed of alternating void and solid prismatic panels.

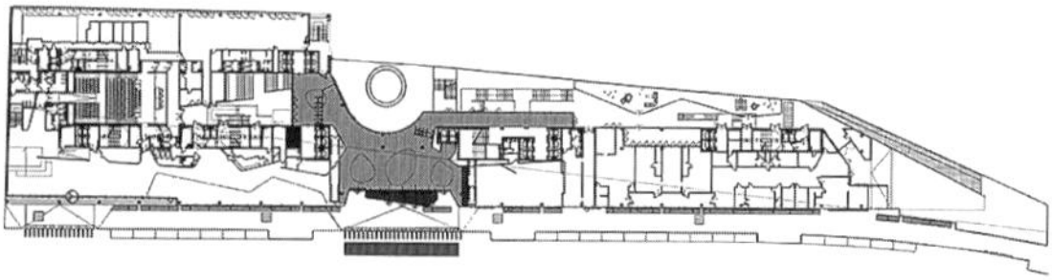

© Gianluca Peluffo&Partners con 5+1AA

© Ernesta Caviola

architects
5+1AA - Alfonso Femia, Gianluca Peluffo

type
offices

construction
2017

60. INA-CASA Tiburtino IV District

Urban development: via Tiburtina km 7
Apartments with external walkways: via Tiburtina, via D. Angeli
Row houses: via dei Crispolti
Tower houses: via D. Angeli, via Luigi Cesana
Terraced houses: via Campotosto, via Rivisondoli
00159 Rome

external viewing only

AV / REG > Stazione Roma Tiburtina

120F / 163 / 211 / nMB > Tiburtina / Cesana

The first example of INA-CASA housing schemes in Rome, coordinated by Mario Ridolfi and Ludovico Quaroni, was based on the concept of creating an authentic village system where the common thread was the connected "street plan". A complex system, but on a human scale where retail shops were concentrated in buildings designed by Ridolfi, and residential buildings were divided into four categories: Apartments with external walkway access (Ridolfi), Tower buildings (Ridolfi), Row houses (Quaroni, Fiorentino), and Terrace houses (Vaccaro, Matauro, Manzone, Palpacelli, Scott Brown husband and wife team). The project is one of the most famous examples of what is considered architectural Neorealism: architecture in the form of modest craftsmanship. An interesting aspect is the external staircase system, that recalls a typically Italian style of "communal living", even when only passing through; in certain cases, the external stairs constitute a true urban element to establish a defined passage. This project can be considered as a construction abacus that summarises all the typical elements of the Italian lifestyle. By using simple methods, architecture can distance itself from the commonplace to become a case study.

architects
Urban development: Ludovico Quaroni, Mario Ridolfi / Apartments with external walkways: Mario Ridolfi / Row houses: Ludovico Quaroni, Mario Fiorentino / Tower houses: Mario Ridolfi / Terraced houses: Giuseppe Vaccaro, Renato Amaturo, Antonino Manzone, Francesco Palpacelli, Denise and Robert Scott Brown

type
residential

construction
Urban development: 1949-1954 / Apartments with external walkways, row and tower houses: 1949-1954 / Terraced houses: 1959-1962

61. Santa Maria Josefa del Cuore di Gesù

via Marcello Candia
00132 Rome

open to the public

+39 06 2248 4432

www.
parrocchiasantamariajosefa.
wordpress.com

With its strong facade composed of solids and voids, the project for the church of Santa Maria Josefa del Cuore di Gesù represents the desire to bring a reference point within a local neighbourhood in order to express the needs of the community. The Garofalo Miura firm created a clean square building, interrupted by an irregular element that houses the weekday chapel. The gently curving profile of the main structure joins the bell tower that seems to be an extension of the main facade. In front of the church entrance is a parvis, and at the rear of the community centre wing, an area for sports activities. The wing is partly raised to house an auditorium-theatre. This project was aimed at redeveloping an area with the inclusion of a public community space within the structure of a place for worship.

051 > Riserva Nuova / Abbateggio

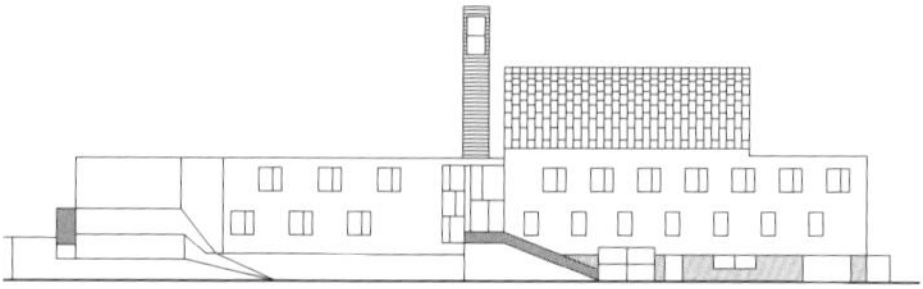

architects
Garofalo Miura Architetti

type
church

construction
1991–2001

62. Chiesa di Dio Padre Misericordioso

piazza largo Terzo Millennio 8
00155 Rome

Mon - Sun /
7.30 am - 7.30 pm

+39 06 231 5833

www.diopadremisericordioso.it

Like a structure that has arrived from the future, the church designed by Richard Meier in 2003 has changed the aspect of the area in which it is located. With its almost unreal whiteness, result of a patented method by Italcementi, the church is the symbol of renewal launched by Pope John Paul II combined with Meier's design, where the iconic and functional are united in a sacred space. The project can be separated into two elements within the triangular site: the sail structures, and the plainer geometrical blocks, designed almost as a plain simple counterbalance alongside the expressive impact of the curved elements. The architects devised an interesting way to introduce light into the liturgical space: light filters inside almost unexpectedly between the sail curves. A magic effect that affects both the faithful and those who are not religious, because beauty captures the heart of one and all.

556 / 556F >
Tovaglieri / Olcese

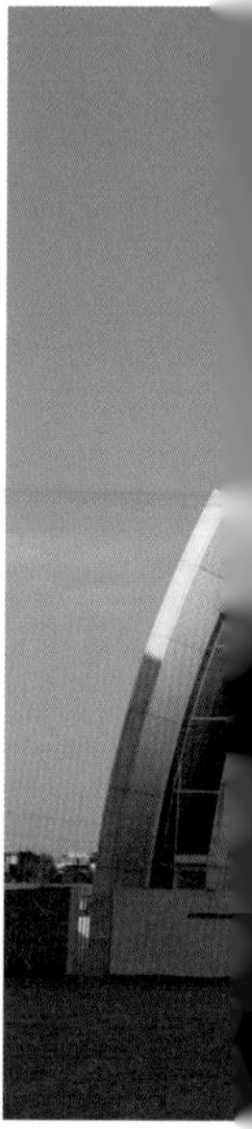

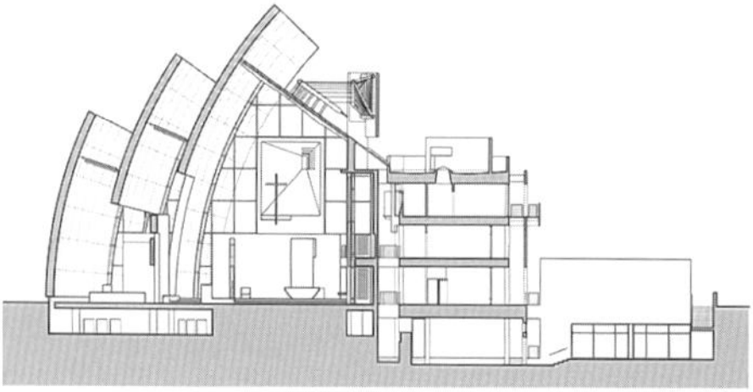

architects
Richard Meier & Partners

type
church

construction
2003

63. Basilica di San Giovanni Bosco

viale dei Salesiani 9
00175 Rome

Mon - Sat / 7 am - 7.30 pm
Sun / 7 am - 8.45 pm

+39 06 710 401 235
donbosco-parrocosdb@
donbosco.it
www.parrocchiadonbosco.it

502 > Salesiani / Pedio

"Give me souls and take the rest" is the Latin motto carved over the central entrance to the Basilica di San Giovanni Bosco, designed by Gaetano Rapisardi. The project was the result of a competition by invitation, created to integrate with the facades of the surrounding high rise residential buildings: a monumental concept to provide continuity between the piazza and the apartment buildings. Inside the church are two domes: one almost 40 metres in diameter, a little smaller than that of the Pantheon and the dome of St. Peter's. It is decorated with marble mosaics, but the most interesting element is the series of multi-coloured windows by Marcello Avenali, Lorenzo Bigotti, Bruno Saetti, Rolando Monti, Virgilio Guzzi and Luigi Montanarini.

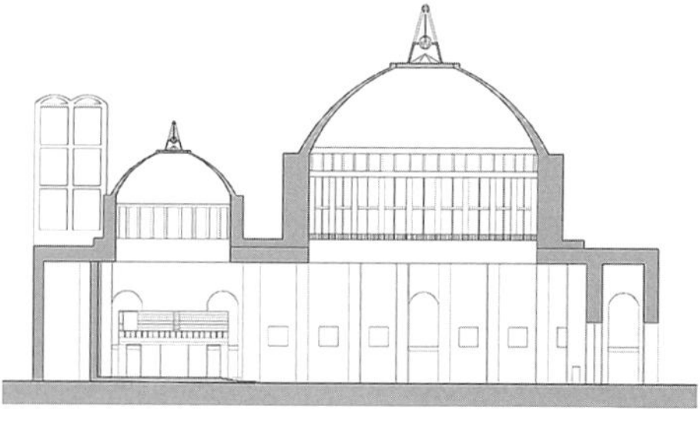

architects
Gaetano Rapisardi

type
church

construction
1959

64. Cinecittà Film Studios

via Tuscolana 1055
00173 Rome

Mon - Sun /
9.30 am - 6.30 pm
Tue / closed

+39 06 722861

www.cinecittastudios.it

A > Cinecittà

213 / 502 / 520 / 654 / 789 / C11 / T02 / nMA > Tuscolana / Cinecittà

The Cinecittà Studios are the iconic hub of Italian cinema and renowned for the famous films that have been shot there. The architect, Gino Peressutti designed a formal enclosure to protect the filming lots to permit far more efficient film shooting. It is an autonomous area, distinct from the surrounding district and is based on simple elements to ensure maximum expression for the art form it produces. The layout is similar to an industrial town, composed of huge rectangular studio hangars with connecting routes and open squares. The aim of the architect was to create a dynamic space without a specific style, allowing it to remain intact and leave it free for future film-making to construct its own image according to evolving technology.

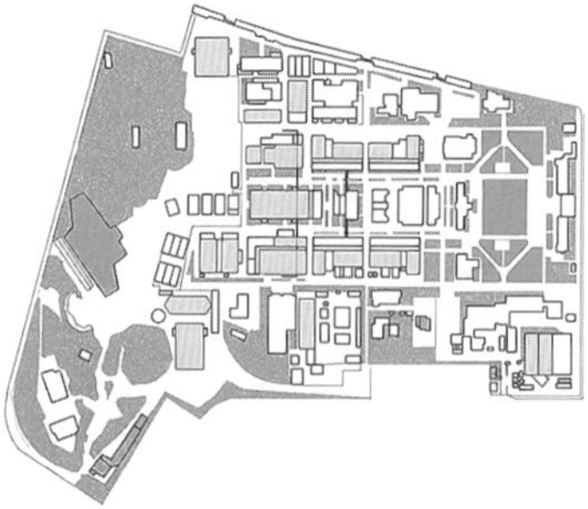

architects
Gino Peressutti

type
film laboratories, offices

construction
1936-1937

65. Hydrobiological Laboratories

via Cracovia 1
00133 Rome

external viewing only

506 > Passolombardo / Cracovia

Winner of the Gold Medal for Italian Architecture in 2006, this project by IaN+ for the new research laboratories of the hydro-biological station of Tor Vergata university, is located in a semi-rural area amid ex-farm buildings that have been converted as departments for the university. The external facing in a brick-coloured, rough-cast finish integrates with the surrounding rural style houses and buildings. The plain rectangular shape was 'bent' in an upward direction to create a large projecting conference space over the main entrance. The two lower floors house the research laboratories. The interior and exterior architectural composition is composed of a system of solids and voids that can be seen in the facades with tall narrow openings on one side, and the long glass window on the upper floor. The unusual angled section on the parallelepiped form, and the cleverly detailed internal layout has created a small but very functional contemporary structure.

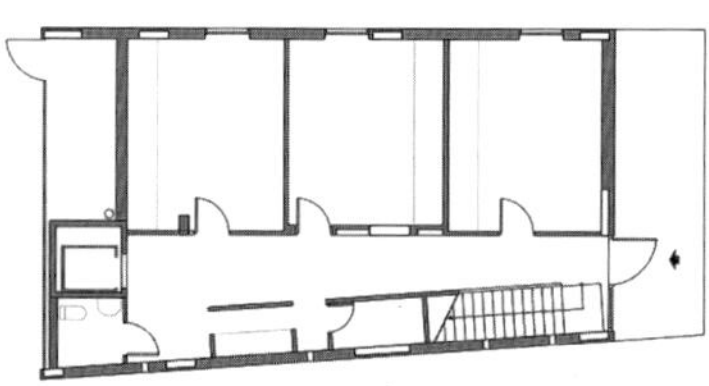

architects
IaN+ (Arch. Carmelo Baglivo,
Arch. Luca Galofaro,
Ing. Stefania Manna)

type
research centre

construction
1998-2004

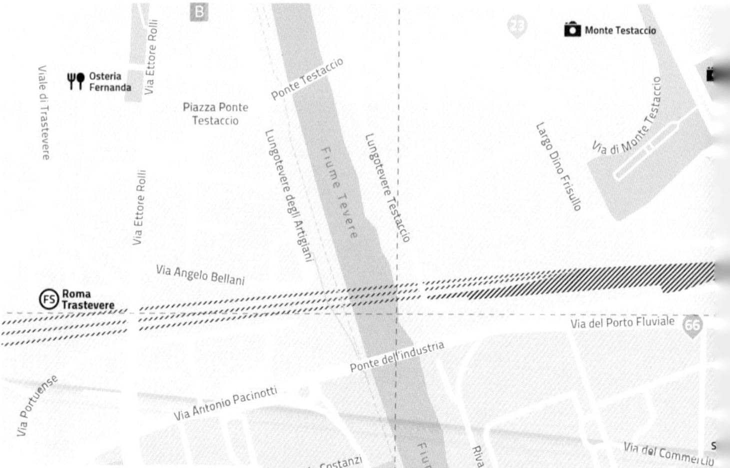

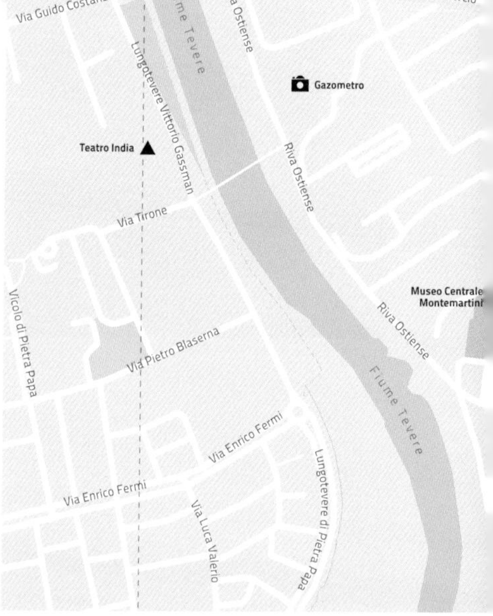

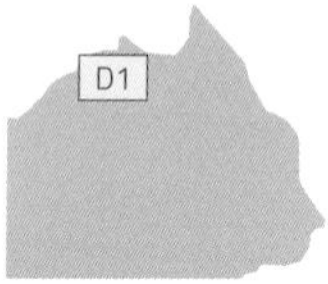

South Rome

66. Opificio RomaEuropa
67. Staging the Museo Centrale Montemartini
68. Ponte Settimia Spizzichino
69. Ardeatine Massacre Memorial Monument
70. Giustiniano Imperatore Urban Redevelopment
71. Chiesa del Santo Volto di Gesù
72. Corviale Housing Project
73. Exxon Buildings at EUR
74. Palazzo della Civiltà Italiana
75. Sturzo Business Centre

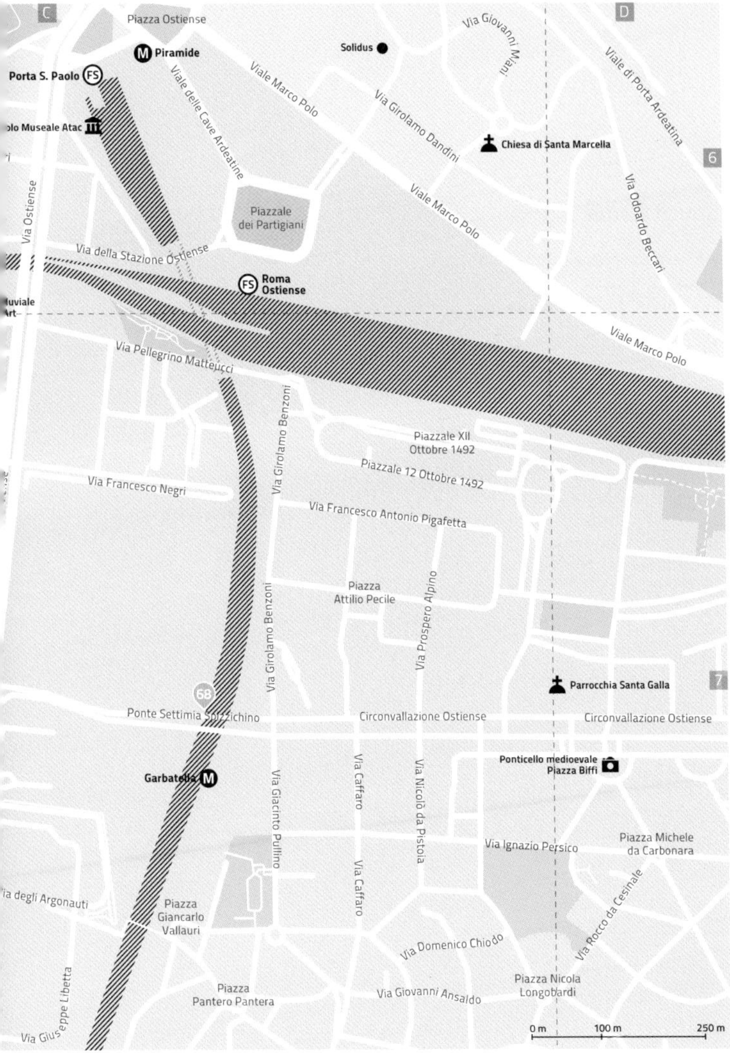

C
D
6
7
Piazza Ostiense
Piramide
Porta S. Paolo
Solidus
Via Giovanni Miani
Viale di Porta Ardeatina
Viale Marco Polo
Via Girolamo Dandini
Viale delle Cave Ardeatine
Polo Museale Atac
Chiesa di Santa Marcella
Via Ostiense
Piazzale dei Partigiani
Via Odoardo Beccari
Via della Stazione Ostiense
Roma Ostiense
Viale Marco Polo
Via Pellegrino Matteucci
Via Girolamo Benzoni
Piazzale XII Ottobre 1492
Piazzale 12 Ottobre 1492
Via Francesco Negri
Via Francesco Antonio Pigafetta
Piazza Attilio Pecile
Via Prospero Alpino
Parrocchia Santa Galla
68
Ponte Settimia Spizzichino
Circonvallazione Ostiense
Circonvallazione Ostiense
Ponticello medioevale Piazza Biffi
Garbatella
Via Giacinto Pullino
Via Caffaro
Via Nicolò da Pistoia
Via Ignazio Persico
Piazza Michele da Carbonara
Via degli Argonauti
Piazza Giancarlo Vallauri
Via Rocco da Cesinale
Via Domenico Chiodo
Via Giuseppe Libetta
Piazza Pantero Pantera
Via Giovanni Ansaldo
Piazza Nicola Longobardi
0 m
100 m
250 m

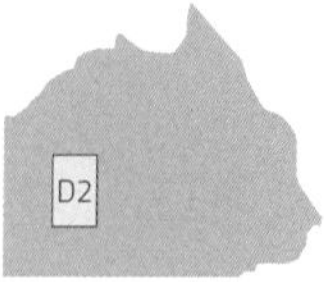

South Rome

76. Palazzo dei ricevimenti e dei congressi
77. Museum of Roman Civilisation
78. The Cloud Convention Centre
79. INAIL Headquarters
80. Enterprise Spa
81. PalaEur Sports Arena
82. Groupama Insurance Headquarters
83. The Engie Building
84. Eurosky Tower
85. Elsa Morante Cultural Centre – Laurentina Library
86. IBM Headquarters Rome

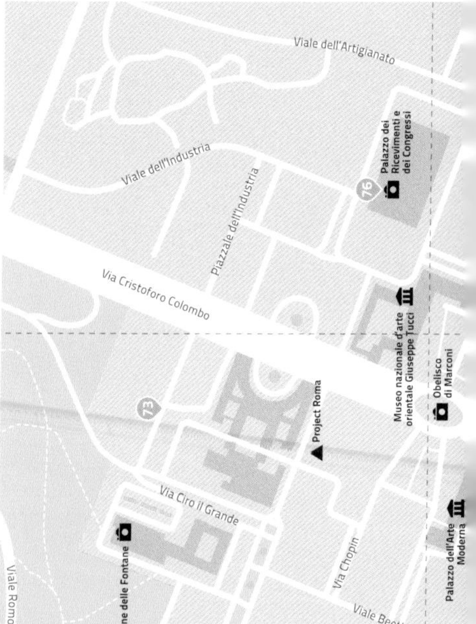
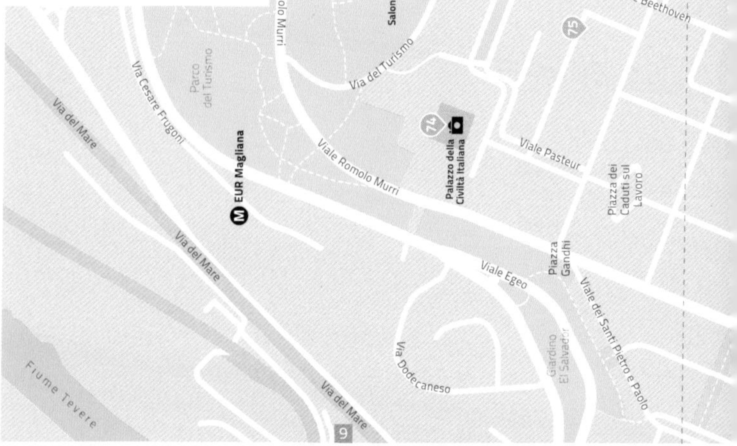

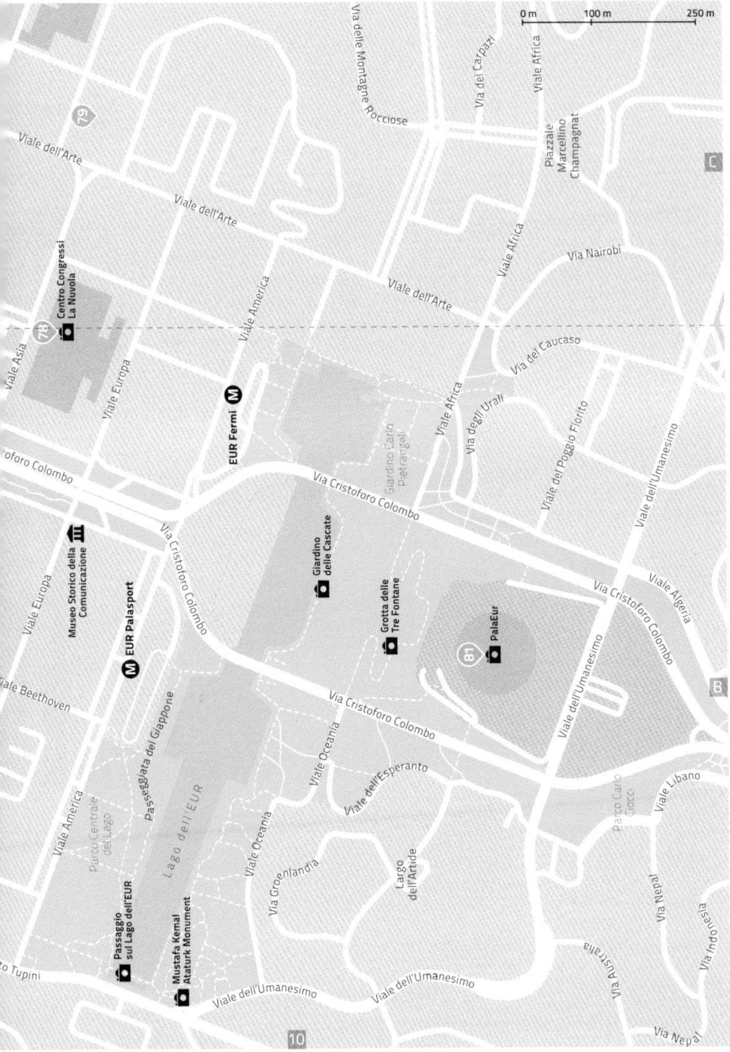
0 m
100 m
250 m
Via delle Montagne Rocciose
Via dei Carpazi
Viale Africa
Piazzale Marcellino Champagnat
C
Viale dell'Arte
Viale dell'Arte
Viale dell'Arte
79
Via Nairobi
Viale Africa
Centro Congressi La Nuvola
78
Viale Asia
Viale America
Viale Europa
EUR Fermi
Via del Caucaso
Via degli Urali
Viale Africa
Giardino Carlo Pietrangeli
Viale del Poggio Fiorito
Viale dell'Umanesimo
Via Cristoforo Colombo
Via Cristoforo Colombo
Museo Storico della Comunicazione
Giardino delle Cascate
Grotta delle Tre Fontane
PalaEur
81
Viale Europa
EUR Palasport
Via Cristoforo Colombo
Viale Algeria
Via Cristoforo Colombo
Viale dell'Umanesimo
B
Viale Beethoven
Passeggiata del Giappone
Via Cristoforo Colombo
Viale Oceania
Viale dell'Esperanto
Lago dell'EUR
Viale America
Parco Centrale del Lago
Viale Oceania
Largo dell'Artide
Parco Carlo Giocco
Viale Libano
Via Groenlandia
Passaggio sul Lago dell'EUR
Mustafa Kemal Ataturk Monument
Via Nepal
Via Indonesia
Via Australia
Viale dell'Umanesimo
Viale dell'Umanesimo
Via Nepal
10

66. Opificio RomaEuropa

via dei Magazzini Generali 20/A
00144 Rome

Mon / 2 pm - 5 pm
Tue - Fri / 10 am - 1 pm,
2 pm - 5 pm
Sat - Sun / closed

+39 06 4555 3050
promozione@romaeuropa.net
fondazioneromaeuropa@pec.romaeuropa.net
www.romaeuropa.net/opificio

B / B1 > Piramide

FL3 / IC / ICN / REG / RV > Roma Ostiense

23 / 769 / nMB / nME > Ostiense / Mercati Generali

Opificio RomaEuropa, headquarters of the foundation by the same name, is a 20th century industrial building that housed a wool processing plant. The architect Andrea Felice converted the building into a flexible modular space, able to cater to a wide range of cultural functions: it hosts performances, conferences, events, workshops, projections in an open airy 1,300 square meter space arranged over two floors. One 150 square metre area provides audience space before a huge projection screen, while another houses logistics services. The steel and glass structure over the old cobblestoned entrance has modernised the previous factory space, creating a functional high quality environment. The glass sloped roofing floods both internal floors with light thanks to long sections cut into the floor slabs and paved with heavy duty glass.

© Andrea Felice

architects
Andrea Felice

type
cultural centre

construction
2008

67. Staging the Museo Centrale Montemartini

via Ostiense 106
00144 Rome

Tue - Sun / 9 am - 7 pm
Mon / closed

+39 06 0608

www.centralemontemartini.org

B / B1 > Garbatella

23 / 792 / nMB / nME
> Ostiense/Garbatella

One of the most interesting aspects when viewing an exhibition is to observe how the art works are arranged in the space. When staging the Museo Centrale Montemartini, architect Francesco Stefanori not only underlined the value of the works on display, but also emphasised the importance of the building housing the exhibits. In this case, the museum is a former thermal power station, and the project is focused on creating a link between the power plant machinery, and the sculpture on show. The exhibits are spread over two floors and the aim is to constantly create a contrast between the ancient sculptures and the industrial archaeology in the plant. This approach creates a powerful, surreal atmosphere, reinforcing the dual image of the machinery and the works of art, merging them into a single concept that summarises man's capacity to create multifaceted art.

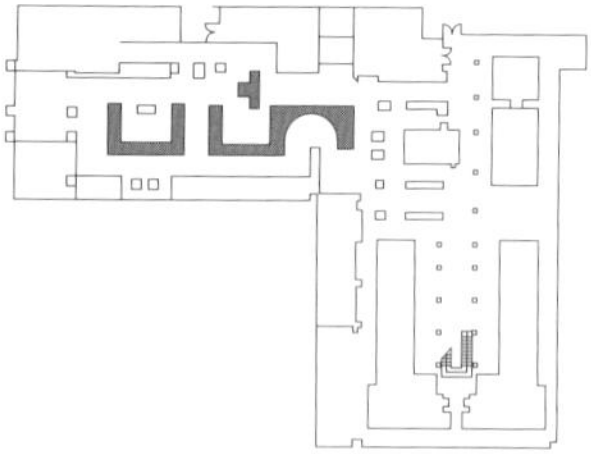

architects
Francesco Stefanori

type
museum

construction
1997

68. Ponte Settimia Spizzichino

Ponte Settimia Spizzichino
00154 Rome

external viewing only

B / B1 > Garbatella

Named after the only survivor of the Roman Jewish Ghetto round-up in 1943, the Ponte Settimia Spizzichino connects the Garbatella district with the ancient Roman road, via Ostiense. The lattice structure was designed by engineer, Francesco del Tosto, and is composed of a suspended arch held by steel cables. As well as the complexity of the structure, the bridge has become an important urban passage, because it is not confined to vehicular traffic, but also includes cycling and foot paths, providing an overpass over the railway lines. Its link with industrial archaeology is the connecting thread of the project; its design has close ties with the surrounding area: the former general markets, old gasometers, and the Montemartini power station. The structural elements are linked with the local context while providing a contemporary high-tech image to the overpass.

architects
Francesco del Tosto

type
bridge

construction
2009-2012

69. Ardeatine Massacre Memorial Monument

via Ardeatina 174
00179 Rome

Mon - Fri / 8.15 am - 3.30 pm
Sat - Sun / 8.15 am - 4.30 pm

+39 06 6783114
info@
mausoleofosseardeatine.it
www.
mausoleofosseardeatine.it

218 > Ardeatina / Fosse Ardeatine
118 > Catacombe S. Callisto

The monument to the martyrs of the Ardeatine Caves was designed to commemorate one of the most terrible massacres of World War Two in Italy, on March 24th, 1944. A competition launched to create a memorial monument was won by two groups of architects. The sunken tuff quarry chamber that holds the 335 tombs is covered by a vast single reinforced concrete slab, like a massive tombstone, supported by six pillars clad in porphyry from the Trento region. The slab is set at a height of about 1.5 metres to create a sombre half-light inside the rectangular space excavated for the burial chamber, with stone walls and floor. The effect of solemn gravitas is achieved through the play in perspective to give the vast geometrical slab an impression of floating above the chamber. The space between the upper edge of the wall around the whole perimeter, and the intrados of the massive covering slab, creates shafts of light but conveys an extremely sombre feeling of oppression. The burial chamber is equipped with rainwater drainage and a ventilation system to compensate the changes in temperature inside the monument.

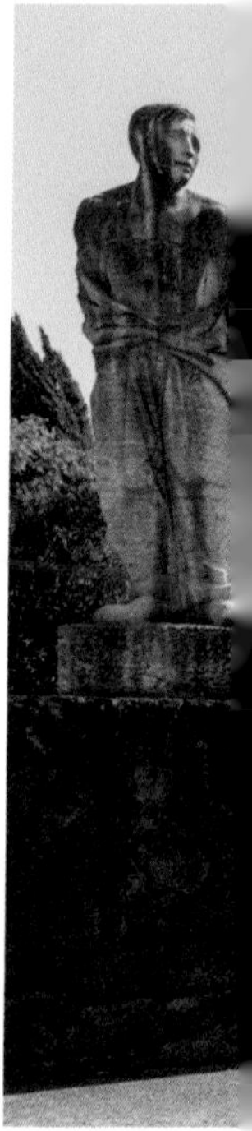

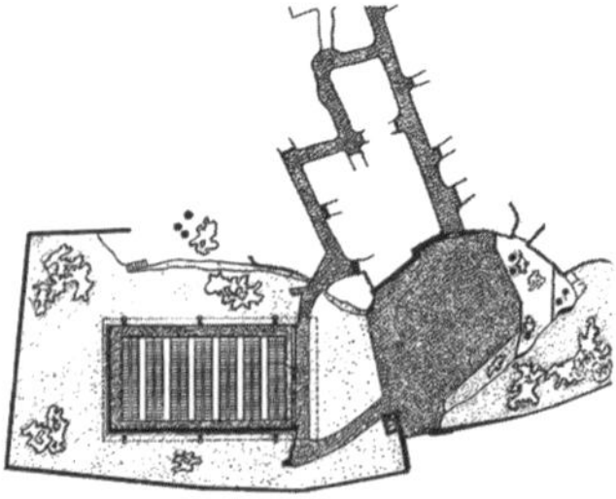

architects
Nello Aprile, Cino Calcaprina, Aldo Cardelli, Mario Fiorentino, Giuseppe Perugini

type
monument

construction
1944-1949

70. Giustiniano Imperatore Urban Redevelopment

viale Giustiniano Imperatore 169
00145 Rome

external viewing only

669 / 766 / 769 / C8
> Giustiniano / Villa Lucina

The Giustiniano Imperatore urban redevelopment programme involved the demolition of several 1950s and 60s buildings in bad condition, and replacing them with new housing, integrating public green spaces and commercial retail areas. The project by ABDR is composed of two buildings, one with a comb structure and the other in butterfly form, built on a common podium base. The building project is divided into two programmed parts: the first relates to the construction of all building structures over 4.5 metres in height, while the second is focused on open spaces, and the bases for the buildings, paying close attention to the obvious compositional contrast like the separation between vertical and horizontal elements, communal and private spaces, urban and residential scales. In the internal courtyard, high circular pillars support the buildings raising them off the ground to increase bioclimatic efficiency. The two buildings enclose a herb garden overlooking the sunken public swimming pool. The residential block facades feature brick and stone vertical bands, interrupted by sun screen shutters to protect the open loggia balconies. Each floor is clearly marked by the exposed string course.

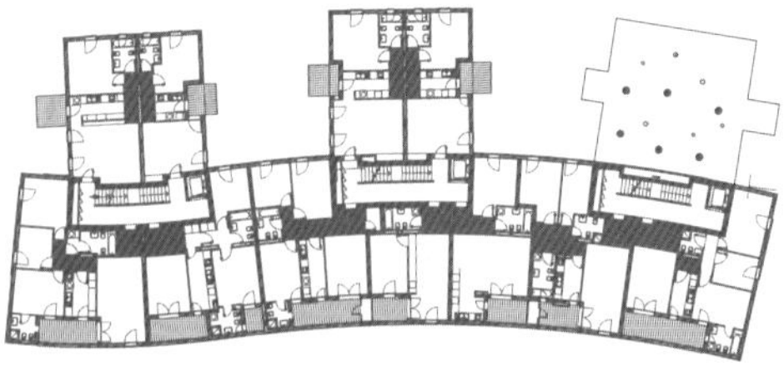

architects
ABDR Architetti Associati

type
residential

construction
2004-2010

71. Chiesa del Santo Volto di Gesù

via della Magliana 162
00146 Rome

Mon - Sun / 8 am - 7.30 pm

+39 06 55 01 063
parrocchia@
parrocchiasantovolto.it
www.parrocchiasantovolto.it

128 / 775 / 780 / 781 / n781 > Magliana / Caprese

The Cross, positioned well beyond the building, is the dominating symbolic and physical point of the project. But it also represents a vanishing point, opening up the parvis like a large "V" in a benign gesture, like two arms reaching towards the city, welcoming the congregation towards the entrance stairs. The vanishing point strategy was used previously in the church of Sant'Ivo by Borromini, with its converging effect and projecting pilasters that circumscribe the concave facade. The lines that define the profiles of the right-hand wing that forms the church crowned with a half-dome, and the left-hand wing housing the parish activities complex, converge in perspective towards the Cross. The internal-external epicentre is composed of a virtual sphere, which appears on the plan as the summation of the external apse and the semi-circular podium with the altar in its centre, separated by a transparent membrane. As a concept of subtraction, the half-dome destined to cover the external space, does not exist: this missing half is represented perceptively by the semi-circular podium where liturgical functions are performed.
The shape of the parvis suggests the concept of the city-community entering the holy space, with its vectoring concept that defines the site between via della Magliana and the adjacent street facing a curve in the Tiber.

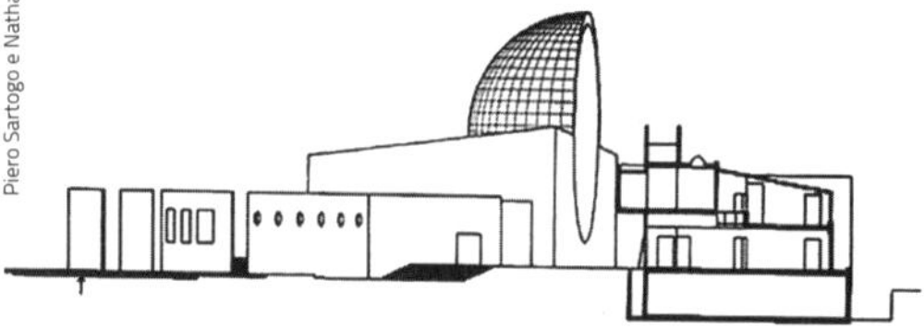

architects
Sartogo Architetti Associati - Piero Sartogo e Nathalie Grenon

type
church

construction
2003-2006

72. Corviale Housing Project

via Poggio Verde 389
00148 Rome

external viewing only

www.corviale.it

98 / 180F / 775 / 786 / 786F / 889 / C7 / M30 / n98 > Poggio Verde / Trentacoste

The "Serpentone" is one of the most ambitious projects assigned to the independent social housing scheme (today called ATER) in 1982, in the via Portuense district. Based on research by Karl Marx-Hof in Vienna, the principles of Le Corbusier's Unité d'Habitation, and projects by Bruno Taut, it is composed of three buildings: two blocks almost a kilometre long and 9 metres high, built opposite one another, connected by five bridges linked with the access entrances. The third building on the west side of the first structure is connected by a bridge. The complex contains 1,200 apartments and original plans included communal areas such as workshops, retail stores and an amphitheatre. The project has always provoked political and public debate and gradually fell into disrepair because of deterioration and mainly because of social change. Today it is a symbol of local renewal development, community participation, and a first architectural redevelopment scheme by Guendalina Salimei. The fourth floor (a free communal zone) is being transformed into communal activity areas, defined with plants and a green patterned band along the facade. A larger regeneration project is underway, by Laura Peretti, winner of the renewal competition in 2015.

architects
Mario Fiorentino, Federico Gorio, Piero Maria Lugli, Giulio Sterbini, Michele Valori / TStudio (Guendalina Salimei) / Laura Peretti Architects

type
residential

construction
1973-1982 / 2009 / 2015-2019

73. Exxon Buildings at EUR

piazzale dell'Agricoltura
00144 Rome

partially open to the public

B / B1 > EUR Magliana

REG > EUR Magliana

788 / C7 > Agricoltura

Known as the "Propylaea of EUR" or "Twin buildings", the Exxon Buildings in the EUR district are two, 50 metre long, T-shaped, structures "placed opposite one another at right angles to via Cristoforo Colombo" to house the Esso and Sgi headquarters. The design is based on the historical layouts of ancient monumental cities, including the high access walls. As well as the three basement floors with a reinforced concrete structure, there are five floors above ground level built on a steel frame 27 metres high. Each block is composed of two right-angled buildings whose architectural composition is based on modules measuring 3 square metres. The regular facade design is composed of three horizontal bands, each with a different type of opening towards the exterior. The first marks the entrance to the building: it is set on pillars and has transparent glass windows; the second, (offices and service areas) has a bronze curtain wall with slightly projecting sun screen slats, while the third, top level has blind walls, and houses the technical systems, creating a separation between the building and the sky.

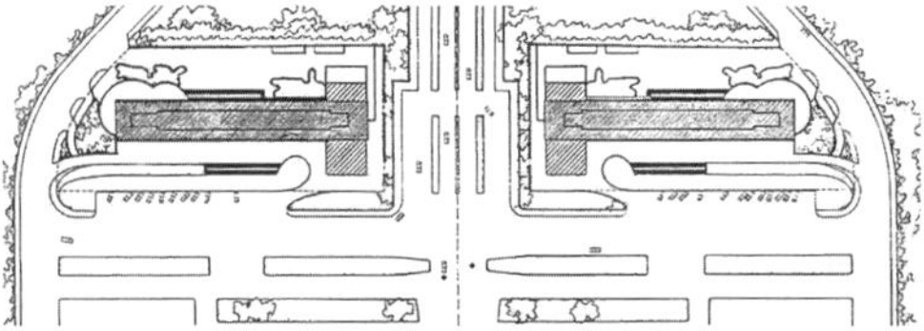

architects
Luigi Moretti, Vittorio Ballio Morpungo, Giovanni Quadarella, Giorgio Sartoro

type
offices

construction
1961-1966

74. Palazzo della Civiltà Italiana

quadrato della Concordia 3
00144 Rome

partially open to the public

www.fendi.com

B / B1 > EUR Magliana

REG > EUR Magliana

31 / 771 / 780 > Tupini / Astronomia

This rationalist monument in modern Rome, the Palazzo della Civiltà Italiana is better known as the Square Colosseum because of the 54 rounded arch openings in the facades. Its presence narrates the concept planned for the 1942 Universal Exposition, as it was one of the first structures built and was chosen as a symbol to celebrate the twentieth anniversary of the Fascist Regime, as well as the urban hub for the route leading to the coast. The structure is a parallelepiped on a square base rising 18 metres above the entrance at street level. Each facade recalls the original concept for the construction of the building with the inscription: "a nation of poets, of artists, of heroes, of saints, of thinkers, of scientists, of navigators, of migrants". At ground level there are 28 statues around the building, allegorically representing various Italian industries, crafts and talents from music to trade, archaeology to law, navigation to military engineering, while four equestrian sculptural groups are placed at the corners. Despite the limits established by MIBAC, the building has been the headquarters of the Fendi Fashion House since 2015.

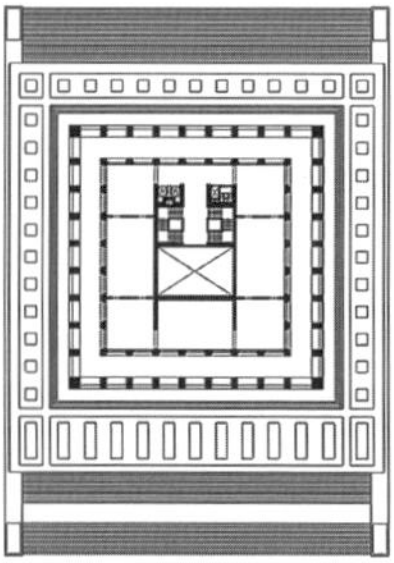

architects
Giovanni Guerrini, Ernesto Lapadula, Mario Romano

type
offices

construction
1939-1953

75. Sturzo Business Centre

piazzale Luigi Sturzo 15
00144 Rome

external viewing only

B / B1 > EUR Palasport

73 / 708 / 762 / 763 / 763L / 764 / 767 / 777 / 779 / 788 / C7 / nMB / nME > Beethoven / Don Sturzo

Sturzo Business Centre was the result of an architectural competition won by Saverio Muratori, for the headquarters of the Christian Democrat party. It is an authentic architectural manifesto, based on the model of historic Roman palaces, both in its facade and layout. Around all four sides of the base podium is a portico providing access to the internal courtyard. The base is slightly recessed in relation to the external facades in order to make the ground level perspective seem lighter and to create a dialogue with its surroundings. The upper floors are a reinterpretation of "historic" Roman palace facades, with far less decorative detailing. The crowning element is composed of a cornice detached from the edge of the top level to create an intriguing play of shadow. The courtyard is the outstanding feature of the building, with regular geometrical openings and projecting cornice that frames the sky above.

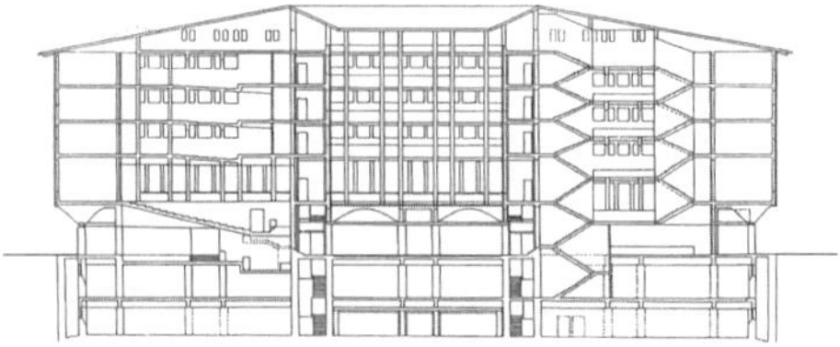

architects
Saverio Muratori

type
offices

construction
1955–1958

76. Palazzo dei ricevimenti e dei congressi

piazza John Kennedy 1
00144 Rome

open to the public

+39 06 5451 3710

This congress building was designed for the 1942 Universal Exposition in the EUR district by Adalberto Libera, and respects the consolidated principles of Fascist Regime architecture. The architect's ideas made it one of the most elegant buildings constructed for the Exposition. An interesting element is the double base podium that leads the viewer towards the discovery of the structure. The first set of stairs leads to the portico, then opens onto the main entrance and then into the "Hall of Culture", a surreal space roofed by a lowered cross-vaulted ceiling with ribbing made from arched metal Vierendeel trusses. Facing piazzale Arte is the congress hall constructed with a series of reinforced concrete frames, while on the second floor is the tiered seating of the open-air theatre. The hall was recently refurbished by the architect Paolo Portoghesi.

B / B1 > EUR Fermi

714 / 791 > Colombo / Marconi

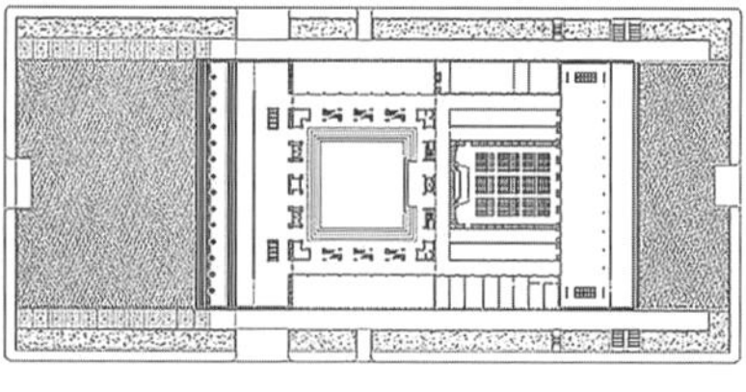

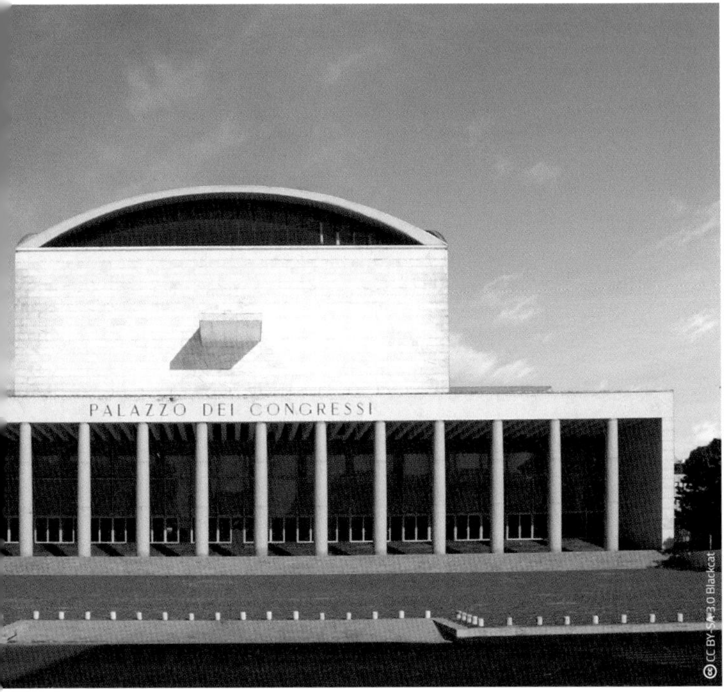

architects
Adalberto Libera

type
auditorium

construction
1937-1942

77. Museum of Roman Civilisation

piazza Guglielmo Marconi 14
00144 Rome

external visits only due to reconstruction work

www.museociviltaromana.it

B / B1 > EUR Fermi

767 / C8 > Museo Civiltà Romana

The Universal Exposition that was to be held in Rome in 1942 provided some of the best examples of Fascist architecture that represent not only a period of history, but also an idea of the magnificence that recalled the Roman Empire. Commissioned by Senator Giovanni Agnelli, the Museum of Roman Civilisation is part of this architectural pattern and many of the design elements underline the style of the period. The base podium gives access to an imposing portico that leads to the two exhibition hall entrances. The colonnade is built in travertine stone, and the decision not to include openings in the facade, using skylights for natural lighting, gives visitors a sensation of true isolation inside the exhibition spaces.

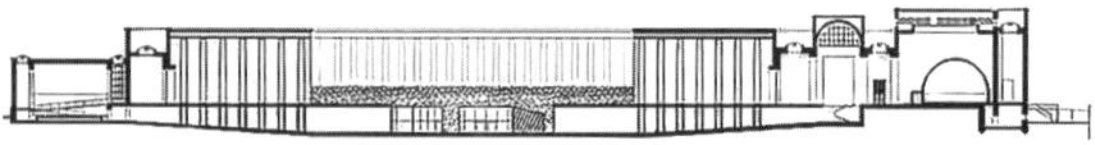

© Luca Farinelli

architects
Pietro Aschieri, Domenico Bernardini, Cesare Pascoletti, Gino Peressutti

type
museum

construction
1939-1952

78. The Cloud Convention Centre

viale Asia 40
00144 Rome

open to the public

+39 06 5451 3710
info@romaconventiongroup.it
www.romaconventiongroup.it

B / B1 > EUR Fermi

30 / 714 / 791 >
Colombo / Europa

The Cloud by Fuksas was an open-air work site for eighteen years. Commissioned with a competition launched in 1998, it finally opened in 2016. The convention centre is based on three concepts that interact with one another: the body of the Cloud, the Theca (Display case) that encloses it, and the Lama (Blade) hotel tower. Coherent with surrounding monumental buildings, the entrance has wide steps that lead up to the information area and open access to the Theca, a metal, glass and reinforced concrete box, created as a public conference area. The congress space is suspended inside the building. It is a Cloud composed of a steel framework covered with a fibreglass and fireproof silicon membrane. The Cloud is attached and supported by a lattice structure. The centre has five interconnected levels that are not associated with any surrounding buildings, as it is designed to be independent in relation to the city. The Lama hotel tower is also separate, with 17 floors, 439 rooms, boutique, spa and restaurant. Anti-seismic and bioclimatic technology complies with all ecological standards for the structures.

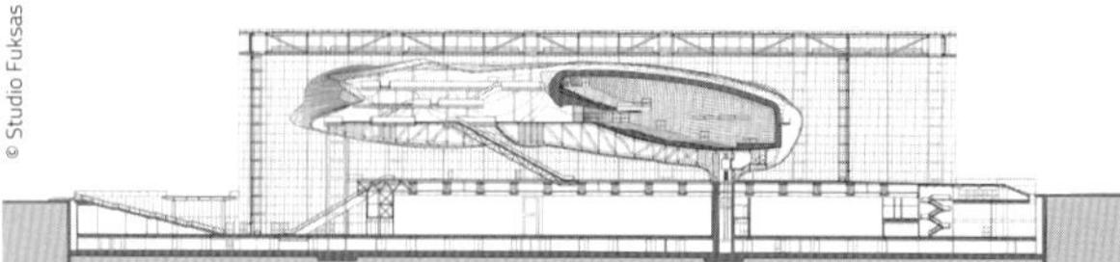

© Studio Fuksas

architects
Studio Fuksas

type
auditorium

construction
2007-2016

79. INAIL Headquarters

piazzale Giulio Pastore 6
00144 Rome

partially open to the public

B / B1 > EUR Fermi

767 / C8 > Museo Civiltà Romana

The new INAIL headquarters is the result of an experimental process conceived in the 1960s, aimed at transferring public services to a single building. Previously known as the Alitalia Tower, then the IBM Building, the INAIL headquarters was completely renovated to respect external safety standards, upgrading the internal structure to 1990s requirements, and making the building coherent with the surrounding context with a travertine base podium. The building has 19 floors and is 72 metres high, and has maintained the blue and white coloured bands on the facade, requested by IBM. The front and back facades are flat, but the sides are curved. As well as spending considerable time eliminating the asbestos from the facades, the architect also changed the building's structure. The long sides of the building were curved to increase and reorganise the internal space to comply with safety standards. This demanded changes in the energy performance, and the building was upgraded with innovative technology spaces.

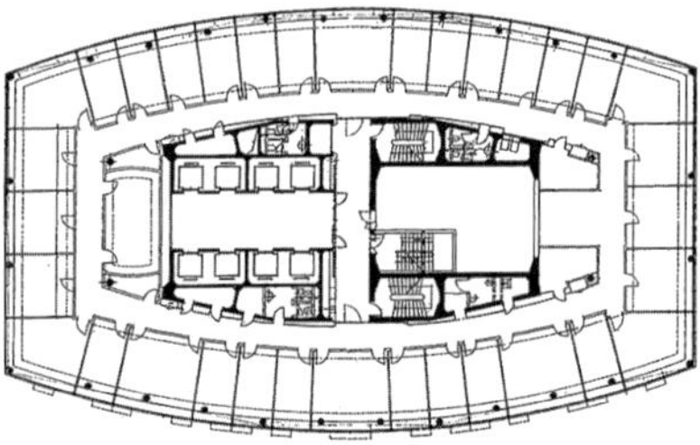

architects
Gino Valle, Cesare Costantini

type
offices

construction
1994

80. Enterprise Spa

viale Egeo 55, via Eufrate 4
00144 Rome

partially open to the public

B / B1 > EUR Palasport

787 / 788 > Egeo / Monte del Finocchio

The new Enterprise Spa headquarters, called "Suspended Spaceship" was built alongside the pre-existing structure, with the entrance from the hilltop to the east, in via Eufrate, close to the Basilica dei Santi Pietro e Paolo. Integrated with the surrounding rationalist landscape, the building strongly expresses the company's innovative spirit. Coherent with the designer's concept, space, form and materials are the leading components. The dominant feature is a projecting structure with a large glass facade providing access to a loggia over the valley, and with a larger floor below, in tuff stone and plaster finish, that follows the line of the pre-existing road retaining walls, below street level. Lighting is discrete, without excessive emphasis, while further light points are positioned in the green park areas and along the external routes. The link between solids and voids, and natural and man-made elements, can also be seen in the various levels that feature platform roofs, walkways, and sun-screens. To compensate the height difference between viale Egeo and the entrance, a monumental travertine staircase provides an architectural solution, set amidst the adjacent spaces designed for relaxation. The dynamic effect perceived from the exterior continues inside where the spaces are flexible, and designed to house contemporary art exhibitions.

© Spazi Multipli

architects
Spazi Multipli

type
offices

construction
2018

81. PalaEur Sports Arena

piazzale Pier Luigi Nervi 1
00144 Rome

open to the public

+39 06 540901
+39 06 488571
info@alleventsspa.it
www.palazzodellosportroma.it

B / B1 > EUR Fermi

780 > Nervi / Palazzo Sport

In 1955, Marcello Piacentini and Pier Luigi Nervi won the competition launched for the construction of a multi-use arena. The circular, 100 metre diameter structure was finished in record time. It was clad in glass and crystal panels, creating plays of light and shadow, concealing the irregular offset internal seating plan. The PalaEur arena is covered with a spherical cap of pre-cast reinforced concrete panels projecting around the perimeter by only nine centimetres and is supported by Y-shaped pillars positioned and blocked by the thrust of the roof panels. The effect suggests monumental supports inserted into the vast internal space. In 1999, the structure was upgraded with restaurants, café-bars and a panoramic terrace, and also underwent maintenance reconstruction to modern safety standards. Massimiliano Fuksas decorated the facade with fluorescent lighting texts that spell out the numbers of the Neapolitan "smorfia" and the name "PalaLottomatica". Today, it is considered one of the most important venues for large events in Europe. The central arena is a modular space that can be adapted to cater to a range of different staged events.

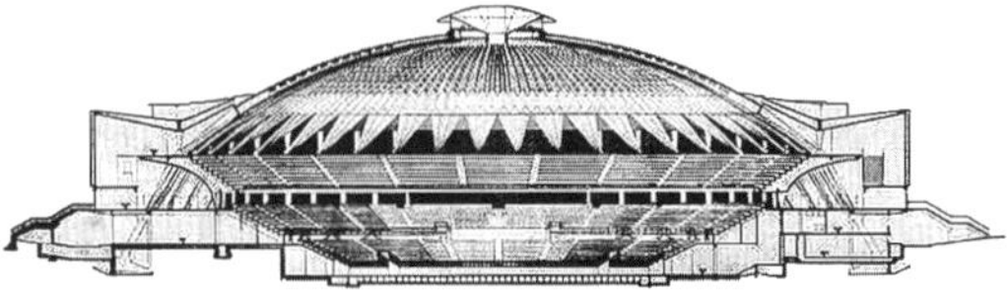

architects
Pier Luigi Nervi,
Marcello Piacentini

type
sports centre

construction
1960

82. Groupama Insurance Headquarters

via Cesare Pavese 385
00144 Rome

partially open to the public

772 / 779 > Pavese / Vittorini

Within the shell built in the 1970s, all internal spaces have been redesigned according to modern comfort standards required for the work-place; the interiors are welcoming, light and mainly focused on an open-space layout to transmit a feeling of solidarity and equality. Circular pillars on one side and a semi-portico on the other define the base of the building. The facades, clad in white micro-perforated sheet metal, feature wider half-pilasters at variable distances from each other to allow light penetration, while other narrower, more regular, closely positioned pilasters create shade where necessary. The white metal pilasters with green and orange methacrylate sides absorb heat in summer and cold in winter. They repeat the dynamic tones inside the building, featured in the partitions, furnishing elements, and cladding materials. Green is the dominant colour in the entrance and surrounding areas, to encourage the public to be aware of nature and the environment. The building is equipped with intelligent technology to improve lighting conditions and reduce electricity consumption.

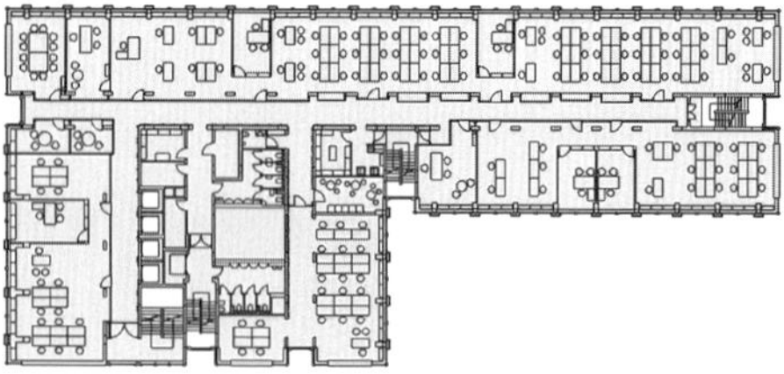

© Studio Transit

architects
Studio Transit

type
offices

construction
2010-2011

83. The Engie Building

viale Giorgio Ribotta 31
00144 Rome

partially open to the public

779 /788 > Tolosa

The Engie company office block is located in the Europarco area. It is an eleven storey rectangular building with a framework constructed on a regular pillar system. The uniform internal concept is repeated on the exterior, beginning with the visible open tower for the emergency stairs, with a span half the width of those used for the framework. The internal play of voids and solids begins in the ground floor entrance as far as the third floor, permitting full access to stairs and elevators. The fourth storey and all floors above it are designed as work spaces. The facade openings have a rectangular geometrical pattern that follows the structural framework, creating a harmonious architectural effect. At the top intersection of two facades, a triangular corner of the building is sliced off, leaving a pyramid-shaped void, above which a single beam emerges to complete the roof profile. The geometrical purity of the building creates a sculptural effect in the local landscape, partly due to the Istria stone cladding on the metal structure that forms the ventilated walls.

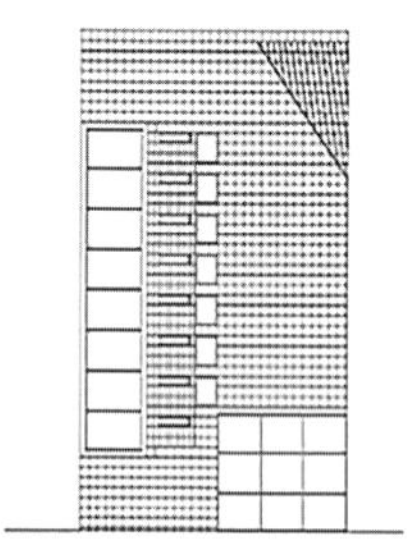

architects
Studio Purini-Thermes

type
offices

construction
2011

84. Eurosky Tower

via Tolosa
00144 Rome

partially open to the public

www.euroskyroma.it

779 /788 > Tolosa

The Eurosky Tower is the symbol of the Europarco master-plan designed by Franco Purini for the Europarco area. Considered the tallest residential building in Italy, 155 metres high, including the antenna, it has become a major landmark in the EUR district. Designed in harmony with the surrounding buildings, it recalls ancient vertical Roman towers. The building is entirely constructed in reinforced concrete and clad in grey granite sheets laid in a regular pattern. Of the 35 storeys, 28 are dedicated to residential use with 200 apartments in a range of 20 different layouts. External terraces are 4 metres deep. Based on Le Corbusier's concept of living, the remaining levels house communal services. The tower has two entrances, a walkway to adjacent public spaces with green parks, and a private walkway below ground level to the garden area.
An exemplary model of ecological architecture, the tower won the Smart Green Building Real Estate Sustainability Award, thanks to internal and external technologies that guarantee the quality required to obtain class A energy standards.

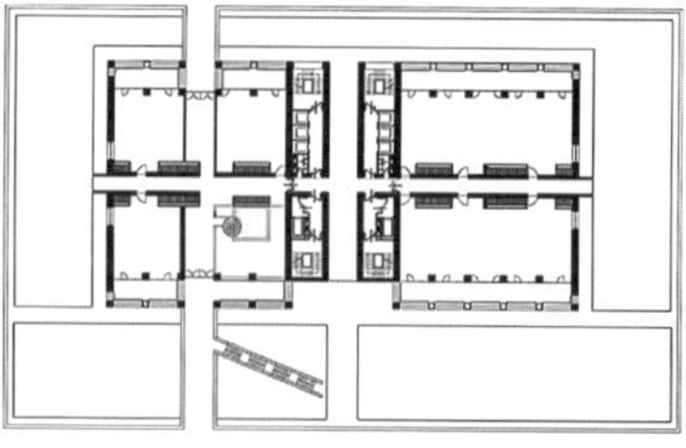

architects
Studio Purini-Thermes

type
offices

construction
2010-2013

85. Elsa Morante Cultural Centre – Laurentina Library

piazza Elsa Morante
00143 Rome

Tue - Thu / 12 am - 7 pm
Fri - Sat / 9 am - 1 pm
Sun / closed

+39 06 4546 0762
laurentina@bibliotechediroma.it ill.laurentina@bibliotechediroma.it
www.bibliotechediroma.it

723 / 779 / n74 >
Silone / Morante

The Elsa Morante cultural centre is a multi-use complex for the community, and is part of the Laurentino 38 redevelopment scheme. Designed as a "local piazza", the centre occupies a natural landscape of almost 5 acres. The horizontal building design is aimed at counteracting the different structural heights so that the ground level is flat, with pedestrian paths, lawns and planted trees, while the structures above ground are supported on slender columns. The complex includes a newspaper and media library, a theatre for 192 spectators, and an arena that can seat 300. The three structures are built parallel to a row of umbrella pine trees, and are designed to remain below the tree canopy. The park also includes a water square, a small wood, and a multimedia piazza, with further common areas located around the main buildings and more closely connected with the Nature Reserve. This is designed to recall the ancient Roman connection between city and countryside. Ecological rainwater collector systems and solar panels provide the centre's irrigation and energy supply.

© Luciano Cupelloni

architects
Luciano Cupelloni

type
library

construction
2005-2010

86. IBM Headquarters Rome

via Luigi Stipa 150
00148 Rome (Ponte Galeria)

partially open to the public

REG > Fiera di Roma

It is not by accident that the last building in this itinerary and in fact, in the whole guide, should be dedicated to one of the most recent buildings constructed in Rome: the new IBM Headquarters.
"It was designed as if it were a landscape": commented studio Z14 to describe the curving sinuous shapes of the various blocks, connected by suspended walkways. The three structures are completely transparent "like an urban lantern", lighting up the surroundings at night. The IBM Headquarters are used as a symbol to indicate the direction towards the Nuova Fiera zone and nearby Roman road, via Portuense, the archaeological digs, and the green park area. This 16 thousand square metres complex provides work space for 1400 employees in an open-space, multi-use environment; the design is highly sustainable, providing comfortable working conditions all year round. The light and airy design and transparent materials almost seem to answer today's social and cultural needs in a large city such as Rome.

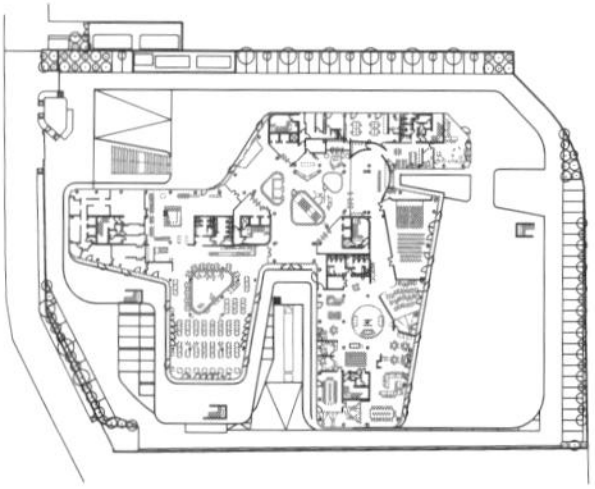

© Studio Z14

architects
Z14 - Alessandro Ridolfi Architetto

type
offices

construction
2019

Museums and Palaces

Accademia di Francia in Villa Medici
Gallery of contemporary art
-
Viale della Trinità dei Monti 1, 00187 Rome

www.villamedici.it
standard@villamedici.it
Tel +39 06 67611

Galleria Corsini
Gallery of ancient art
-
Via della Lungara 10, 00165 Rome

www.barberinicorsini.org
Tel +39 06 68802323

Galleria dell'Accademia di San Luca
Gallery of modern and contemporary art
-
Piazza Accademia di S. Luca 77,
00187 Rome

www.accademiasanluca.eu
Tel +39 06 6798850

Galleria Doria Pamphili
Museum of ancient art
-
Via del Corso 305, 00186 Rome

www.doriapamphilj.it
Tel +39 06 6797323

Galleria Nazionale d'Arte Antica in Palazzo Barberini
Gallery of ancient art
-
Via delle Quattro Fontane 13,
00184 Rome

www.barberinicorsini.org
Tel +39 06 4814591

Galleria Nazionale d'Arte Moderna e Contemporanea
Gallery of modern and contemporary art
-
Viale delle Belle Arti 131, 00197 Rome

www.lagallerianazionale.com
gan-amc@beniculturali.it
Tel +39 06 322981

Museo di Roma in Palazzo Braschi
Museum of modern and contemporary art
-
Museo di Roma, Piazza San Pantaleo 10,
00186 Rome / piazza Navona 2, 00186 Rome

www.museodiroma.it
museodiroma@comune.roma.it
Tel +39 06 0608

Museo Nazionale Etrusco di Villa Giulia
Museum of ancient art
-
Piazzale di Villa Giulia 9, 00196 Rome

www.museoetru.it
mn-etru@beniculturali.it
Tel +39 06 3226571

Museo Nazionale Romano
Museum of modern and ancient art
-
Palazzo Altemps:
piazza di Sant'Apollinare 46, 00186 Rome
Palazzo Massimo alle Terme:
largo di Villa Peretti 2, 00185 Rome
Terme di Diocleziano:
viale Enrico de Nicola 78, 00185 Rome

www.museonazionaleromano.beniculturali.it
mn-rm@beniculturali.it /
mbac-mn-rm@mailcert.beniculturali.it
Tel +39 06 684851

Parco archeologico del Colosseo – Palatino and Domus Aurea
Archaeological site
-
Via di San Gregorio 30, 00186 Rome / via della Domus Aurea 1, 00184 Rome

www.parcocolosseo.it
ssba_rm.infocolosseo@beniculturali.it
Tel +39 06 39967700

Basilicas and Churches

Basilica di San Giovanni in Laterano
Piazza di S. Giovanni in Laterano 4, 00184 Rome

www.vatican.va
basilica@laterano.va
Tel +39 06 69886433 / +39 06 7727991

Basilica di San Lorenzo fuori le Mura
Piazzale del Verano 3, 00185 Rome

www.basilicadisanlorenzo.com
basilicasanlorenzofuorilemura@gmail.com
Tel +39 06 491511

Basilica di San Sebastiano fuori le Mura
Via Appia Antica 136, 00179 Rome

www.sansebastianofuorilemura.org
info@sansebastianofuorilemura.org
Tel + 39 06 7808847

Basilica di Santa Cecilia in Trastevere
Piazza di Santa Cecilia 22, 00153 Rome

www.benedettinesantacecilia.it
monastero@benedettinesantacecilia.it
Tel +39 06 45492739

Basilica di Santa Croce in Gerusalemme
Piazza di S. Croce in Gerusalemme, 00185 Rome

www.santacroceroma.it
info@santacroceroma.it
Tel +39 06 70613053

Basilica di Santa Maria in Ara Coeli
Scala dell'Arce Capitolina 12, 00186 Rome

Tel +39 06 69763839

Basilica di Santa Maria Sopra Minerva
Piazza della Minerva 42, 00186 Rome

www.santamariasopraminerva.it
santamariasopraminerva@gmail.com
Tel +39 06 69920384

Basilica di Santa Prassede
Via di Santa Prassede 9/a, 00184 Rome

www.santaprassede.wordpress.com
basilicas.prassede@libero.it
Tel +39 06 4882456

Basilica di Santo Stefano Rotondo al Celio
Via Santo Stefano Rotondo 7, 00184 Rome

www.romanoimpero.com
Tel +39 06 42119130

Basilica Papale di Santa Maria Maggiore
Piazza di S. Maria Maggiore, 00100 Rome

w2.vatican.va

Chiesa di San Luigi dei Francesi
Piazza di S. Luigi de' Francesi, 00186 Rome

www.saintlouis-rome.net
Tel +39 06 688271

Chiesa di Sant'Ivo alla Sapienza
Corso del Rinascimento 40, 00186 Rome

www.sivoallasapienza.eu
info@sivoallasapienza.eu
Tel +39 06 872901

Chiesa di Santa Maria della Pace
Arco della Pace 5, 00186 Rome
Tel +39 06 68804038

Santuario della Scala Santa e Sancta Sanctorum
Piazza San Giovanni in Laterano 14, 00184 Rome
www.scala-santa.com
scalasantaroma@gmail.com
Tel +39 329 75111

Theatres

Teatro Ambra Jovinelli
Via Gugliemo Pepe 43, 00185 Rome
www.ambrajovinelli.org
segreteria@ambrajovinelli.org
Tel +39 06 83082884 - 06 83082620

Teatro Argentina
Largo di Torre Argentina 52, 00186 Rome
www.teatrodiroma.net
Tel +39 06 684000311 / 14

Teatro Belli
Piazza di Sant'Apollonia 11, 00153 Rome
www.teatrobelli.it
info@teatrobelli.it
Tel +39 06 5894875

Teatro Brancaccio
Via Merulana 244, 00185 Rome
www.teatrobrancaccio.it
botteghino@teatrobrancaccio.it
Tel +39 06 80687231

Teatro dell'Opera
Piazza Beniamino Gigli, 00184 Rome
www.operaroma.it
ufficio.biglietteria@operaroma.it
Tel +39 06 4817003

Teatro Sistina
Via Sistina 129, 00187 Rome
www.ilsistina.it
frontoffice@ilsistina.it
Tel +39 06 4200711

Teatro Torlonia
Via Lazzaro Spallanzani 1A, 00161 Rome
www.teatrodiroma.net
Tel +39 06 684000311 / 14

Restaurants and Trattorias

• • • expensive
• • mid-range
• inexpensive

Antico Forno Roscioli •
Via dei Chiavari 34, 00186 Rome
www.anticofornoroscioli.it
Tel +39 06 6864045

Aroma • • •
Via Labicana 125, 00184 Rome
www.aromarestaurant.it
info@aromarestaurant.it
Tel +39 06 97615109

Felice a Testaccio • •
Via Mastro Giorgio 29, 00153 Rome
www.feliceatestaccio.it
Tel +39 06 5746800

Flavio al Velavevodetto • •
Via di Monte Testaccio, 97, 00153 Rome /
Piazza dei Quiriti 4/5, 00192 Rome
www.ristorantevelavevodetto.it
Tel +39 06 5744194 / +39 06 36000009

Il Marchese – Osteria Mercato Liquori • •
Via di Ripetta 162, 00186 Rome
www.ilmarcheseroma.it
info@ilmarcheseroma.it
Tel +39 06 90218872

Imàgo • • •
Piazza della Trinità dei Monti 6, 00187 Rome
www.hotelhasslerroma.com
imago@hotelhassler.it
Tel +39 06 699 34726

Mordi & Vai •
Nuovo Mercato Comunale di Testaccio,
Via Beniamino Franklin 12/E, 00153 Rome
www.mordievai.it
Tel +39 339 1343344

Osteria Fernanda • • •
Via Crescenzo del Monte 18, 00153 Rome
www.osteriafernanda.com
osteriafernanda@libero.it
Tel +39 06 5894333

Ristorante Il Caminetto • •
Viale dei Parioli 89, 00197 Rome
www.caminettoroma.it
info@caminettoroma.it
Tel +39 06 8083946

Tonnarello • •
Via della Paglia 1, 00153 Rome
www.tonnarello.it
info@tonnarello.it
Tel +39 06 5806404

Hotels

Alessandro Palace Hostel & Bar •
Via Vicenza 42, 00185 Rome
www.hostelsalessandro.com
palace@HostelsAlessandro.com
Tel +39 06 4461958

Generator Rome •
Via Principe Amedeo 251, 00185 Rome
www.staygenerator.com
Tel +39 06 492330

Hotel Hassler Roma • • •
Piazza Trinità dei Monti 6, 00187 Rome
www.hotelhasslerroma.com
info@hotelhassler.it
Tel +39 06 699340

Hotel Residenza in Farnese • • •
Via Del Mascherone 59, 00186 Rome
www.residenzafarneseroma.it
booking@residenzafarneseroma.it
Tel +39 06 68210980

Hotel San Francesco • •
Via Jacopa de' Settesoli 7, 00153 Rome
www.hotelsanfrancesco.net
info@hotelsanfrancesco.net
Tel +39 06 58300051

Hotel San Giovanni • • •
Via Licia 7, 00183 Rome
www.hotelsangiovanniroma.it
info@hotelsangiovanniroma.it
Tel +39 06 64011405

• • • expensive
• • mid-range
• inexpensive

Hotel Teatro Pace • •
Via del Teatro Pace 33, 00186 Rome
www.hotelteatropace.com
info@hotelteatropace33
Tel +39 06 6879075

Nerva Boutique Hotel • •
Via Tor de'Conti 3/4, 00184 Rome
www.hotelnerva.com
info@hotelnerva.com
Tel +39 06 6781835 / +39 06 6793764

Radisson Blu ES Hotel • • •
Via Filippo Turati 171, 00185 Rome
www.radissonhotels.com
info.rome@radissonblu.com
Tel +39 06 444841

The Liberty Boutique Hotel • • •
Via Palestro 64, 00185 Rome
www.hoteltheliberty.com
info@hoteltheliberty.com
Tel +39 06 4959261

The RomeHello •
Via Torino 45, 00184 Rome
www.theromehello.com
ciao@theromehello.com
Tel +39 06 96860070

Architectural offices

ABDR Architetti Associati
Via delle Conce 20, 00154 Rome
www.abdr.it
info@abdr.it
Tel +39 06 57250470-57

Alvisi Kirimoto
Viale Parioli 40, 00197 Rome
www.alvisikirimoto.it
info@alvisikirimoto.it
Tel +39 06 45473803

Andrea Felice Art & Design
Via di Casal Bruciato 11, 00159 Rome
www.andreafelice.eu
Tel +39 06 97843119

Cupelloni Architettura
Via Leopardi 19, 00185 Rome
www.lc-architettura.com
studio@lc-architettura.com
Tel +39 06 4825413

Da Gai Architetti
Via Padre Raffaele Melis 17, 00176 Rome
www.dagaiarchitetti.it
studio@enricodagai.it
Tel +39 06 77590467

Garofalo Miura Architetti
via Nomentana Nuova 111, 00141 Rome
www.garofalomiura.it
info@garofalomiura.it
Tel +39 06 87462580

IaN+
Viale Marco Polo 121, 00154 Rome
www.ianplus.it
ian[at]ianplus.it
Tel +39 06 57300403

Insula architettura e ingegneria
via Ostiense 177/c, 00154 Rome
www.insulainrete.it
insula@insulainrete.it
Tel +39 06 5756182

It's
Via Ignazio Pettinengo 72, 00159 Rome

www.its.vision
info@its.vision
Tel +39 06 87566110

King Rosselli Architetti
Piazza Farnese 44, 00186 Rome

www.kingroselli.com
mail@kingroselli.com
Tel +39 06 68210551

Labics
Via Ennio Quirino Visconti 11, 00193 Rome

www.labics.it
info@labics.it
Tel +39 06 57288049

Laura Peretti Architects
Viale Manzoni 39, 00185 Rome

www.lauraperettiarchitects.com
info@studioinsito.com
Tel +39 06 58334070

Nemesi Studio
Via di Pietralata 159/163, 00158 Rome

www.nemesistudio.it
info@nemesistudio.it
Tel +39 06 45439167-8

Sartogo Architetti Associati
Via Sardegna 14, 00187 Rome

www.sartogoarchitetti.it
press@sartogoarchitetti.it
Tel +39 064457144-145

Solidus
Via Federico Nansen 68, 00154 Rome

www.solidusroma.com
segreteria@solidusroma.it
Tel +39 06 57250554

Studio Fuksas
Piazza del Monte di Pietà 30, 00186 Rome

www.fuksas.com
office@fuksas.com
Tel +39 06 68807871

Studio Kami
Via di Pietralata 157, 00158 Rome

www.studiokami.it
info@studiokami.it
Tel + 39 06 4180404

Spazi Multipli
Via Amerigo Vespucci 26, 00153 Rome

www.multipli.it
info@multipli.it
Tel +39 06 5782614

Studio Passarelli
Via Campania 59, 00187 Rome

www.studiopassarelli.it
studiopassarelli@studiopassarelli.it
Tel +39 06 94358033

Studio Purini-Thermes
Via Tagliamento 55, 00198 Rome

franco.purini@virgilio.it / thermes@tin.it
Tel +39 06 85355047

Studio Transit
Via del Commercio 12 (cortile dx), 00154 Rome

www.studiotransit.it
studiotransit@studiotransit.it
Tel +39 06 5899893

Studio Z14, Alessandro Ridolfi
Via Cassia 994, 00187 Rome

www.studioz14.it
a.ridolfi@studioz14.it
Tel +39 06 30366688

T-Studio
Piazza Antonio Mancini 4, 00196 Rome

www.tstudio.net
Tel + 39 06 3235197

Index by architect

Index by project

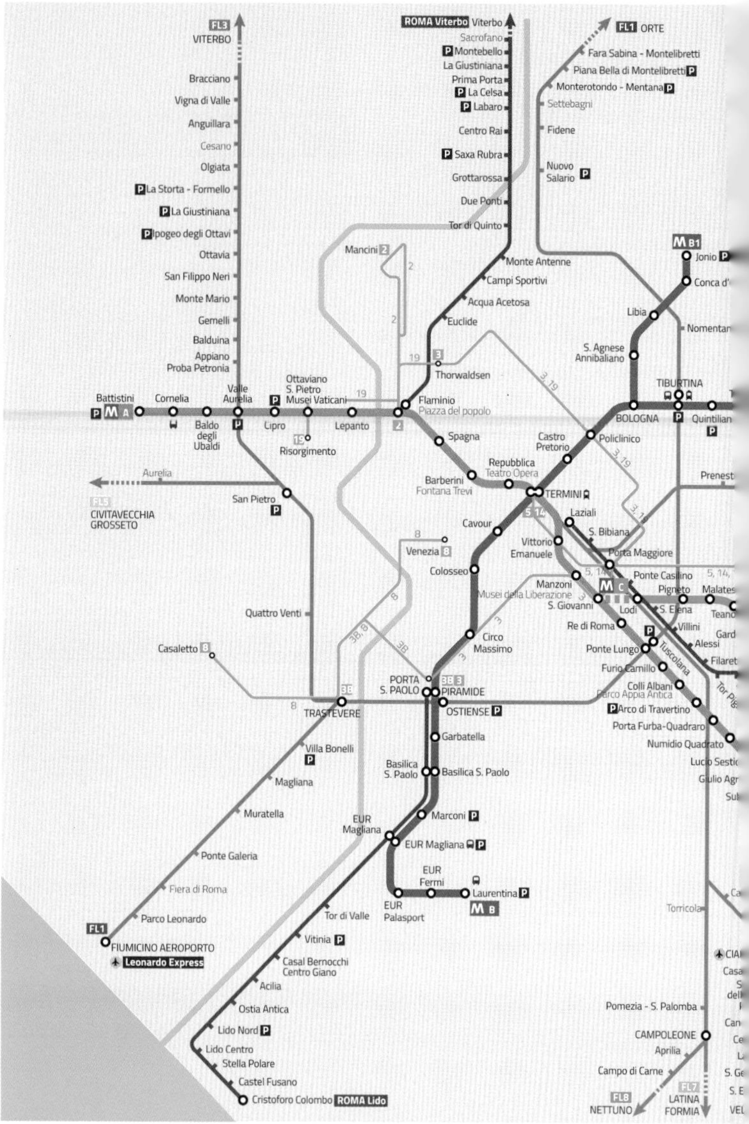

FL3
VITERBO
Bracciano
Vigna di Valle
Anguillara
Cesano
Olgiata
La Storta - Formello
La Giustiniana
Ipogeo degli Ottavi
Ottavia
San Filippo Neri
Monte Mario
Gemelli
Balduina
Appiano
Proba Petronia
ROMA Viterbo
Viterbo
Sacrofano
Montebello
La Giustiniana
Prima Porta
La Celsa
Labaro
Centro Rai
Saxa Rubra
Grottarossa
Due Ponti
Tor di Quinto
Monte Antenne
Campi Sportivi
Acqua Acetosa
Euclide
FL1
ORTE
Fara Sabina - Montelibretti
Piana Bella di Montelibretti
Monterotondo - Mentana
Settebagni
Fidene
Nuovo
Salario
Mancini
M B1
Jonio
Libia
S. Agnese
Annibaliano
Nomentan
TIBURTINA
BOLOGNA
Quintilian
Thorwaldsen
Battistini
Cornelia
Baldo
degli
Ubaldi
Valle
Aurelia
Cipro
Ottaviano
S. Pietro
Musei Vaticani
Lepanto
Flaminio
Piazza del popolo
Risorgimento
Spagna
Castro
Pretorio
Policlinico
Repubblica
Teatro Opera
Barberini
Fontana Trevi
TERMINI
Prenest
Aurelia
FL5
CIVITAVECCHIA
GROSSETO
San Pietro
Cavour
Laziali
S. Bibiana
Vittorio
Emanuele
Porta Maggiore
Venezia
Colosseo
Manzoni
Musei della Liberazione
S. Giovanni
Ponte Casilino
Pigneto
Malates
Lodi
S. Elena
Teano
Quattro Venti
Re di Roma
Villini
Gard
Alessi
Filaret
Casaletto
Circo
Massimo
Ponte Lungo
Tuscolana
Furio Camillo
Colli Albani
Parco Appia Antica
Tor Pig
PORTA
S. PAOLO
PIRAMIDE
TRASTEVERE
OSTIENSE
Arco di Travertino
Porta Furba-Quadraro
Numidio Quadrato
Lucio Sestio
Giulio Agr
Sub
Garbatella
Villa Bonelli
Magliana
Basilica
S. Paolo
Basilica S. Paolo
Muratella
EUR
Magliana
Marconi
EUR Magliana
Ponte Galeria
Fiera di Roma
EUR
Fermi
Laurentina
EUR
Palasport
M B
Parco Leonardo
Tor di Valle
Torricola
FL1
FIUMICINO AEROPORTO
Leonardo Express
Vitinia
Casal Bernocchi
Centro Giano
Acilia
Ostia Antica
Pomezia - S. Palomba
Lido Nord
Lido Centro
Stella Polare
Castel Fusano
CAMPOLEONE
Aprilia
Campo di Carne
Cristoforo Colombo
ROMA Lido
FL8
NETTUNO
FL7
LATINA
FORMIA